# Silver & Gold

# Silver & Gold

## Cased Images of the California Gold Rush

*Edited by* **Drew Heath Johnson** *&* **Marcia Eymann**

*Published by the* University of Iowa Press *for the* Oakland Museum of California

*This book is published in conjunction with the exhibition "Silver & Gold: Cased Images of the California Gold Rush," curated by Drew Heath Johnson and Marcia Eymann, presented by the Oakland Museum of California, Oakland, California, January 24, 1998 (the 150th anniversary of the discovery of gold in California), to July 26, 1998. The second venue is the National Museum of American Art, Smithsonian Institution, Washington, D.C., October 30, 1998, to March 7, 1999. The third venue is the Crocker Art Gallery, Sacramento, California, August 13, 1999, to October 10, 1999.*

*This publication and exhibition have been funded as follows.*
*Presenting Sponsors: Oakland Museum Women's Board, Clorox Company Foundation, and Anonymous.*
*Major Sponsors: Barkley Fund, Walter and Elise Haas Fund, Kaiser Permanente, Wells Fargo, S. H. Cowell Foundation, Levi Strauss Foundation, Bernard Osher Foundation, Pacific Gas and Electric Company, Rockefeller Foundation, and L. J. Skaggs and Mary C. Skaggs Foundation.*
*Contributing Sponsors: Richard and Rhoda Goldman Fund, Oakmead Foundation, Mr. and Mrs. Ellis Stephens, Union Bank of California, David and Lyn Anderson, Crosby Heafey Roach & May, Helen F. Novy, Dr. Albert Shumate, William F. Weeden, and other members and friends of the Oakland Museum of California.*

University of Iowa Press,
Iowa City 52242
Copyright © 1998 by the
University of Iowa Press
All rights reserved
Printed in the United States of America
Design by Richard Hendel
http://www.uiowa.edu/~uipress

Printed on acid-free paper
Library of Congress
Cataloging-in-Publication Data
Silver & gold: cased images of the California
   gold rush / edited by Drew Heath Johnson and
   Marcia Eymann.
      p.    cm.
   Includes bibliographical references.
   ISBN 0-87745-619-4, ISBN 0-87745-620-8 (pbk.)
   1. California—Gold discoveries—Pictorial
works—Exhibitions.   2. California—Social
life and customs—19th century—Pictorial
works—Exhibitions.   3. Daguerreotype—
California—Exhibitions.   I. Johnson, Drew
Heath.   II. Eymann, Marcia.   III. Oakland
Museum of California.   IV. National Museum
of American Art (U.S.).   V. E. B. Crocker Art
Gallery.
   F865.S555   1998
   979.4′04—DC21                              97-31402

98  99  00  01  02  C  5  4  3  2  1
98  99  00  01  02  P  5  4  3  2  1

*Dedicated to the daguerreians, argonauts, and collectors—pioneers all*

# Contents

# Preface

## *Therese Thau Heyman*

*Even with out asking,*
*California's precious earth,*
*Turns the new world frantic,*
*Sell your traps, and take a birth* [sic]
*Across the wild Atlantic.*
*Every one who digs and delves,*
*All whose arms are brawny,*
*Take a pick and help yourselves —*
*Off to Californy*
— "Digging Gold," c. 1854

An illustrated broadside sheet, "Digging Gold" voiced the exhilarating clarion call to action and adventure — to abandon old ways and join the rush for California's gold. Surely the wonder of this amazing and defining event had to be recorded and collected by the Oakland Museum of California, as the museum's regional focus demanded paying significant attention to the earliest photographs of the West. To begin such a collection — my first assignment when I arrived as curator in 1961 — seemed a challenge but in fact proved to be a timely opportunity to seek out the great, still available collections that would soon become impossible to acquire.

California's far-seeing photographers led the way in this effort, supporting the goal to build the best of California art photography collections. Ansel Adams, the first to respond, contributed advice and landmark photographs, then Dorothea Lange and Paul Taylor endorsed the program, offering generous gifts that eventually became the Dorothea Lange Archive. Happily, Stanley Truman and Dudley Bell, skilled amateur photographers themselves, understood the need to purchase important nineteenth-century images and successfully raised substantial funds for us. Through an Oakes Foundation grant, a handsome oak-paneled storage area, a study room, and a gallery provided a home for photographs and works on paper within the previously unfinished art department.

Supported by these significant resources, we sought out the images that defined photography and introduced West Coast image makers. Among the cased images we received was the startlingly clear half plate daguerreotype of William Shew's wheeled daguerreian wagon, parked in San Francisco and advertising its wares with a row of tiny, yet still legible daguerreotypes displayed along a ledge on the wagon's side to lure and captivate customers (pl. 149). Through purchase we acquired a splendid six-part daguerreian panorama of San Francisco (pl. 34), and as an important addition to city views, we obtained the whole plate view of beautiful South Park, fashionable in its day, and even today remarkably unchanged (pl. 138).

*Attributed to William Shew (1820–1903)*
**Shew's Daguerreian Saloon and the *Alta California* Newspaper Office,**
**San Francisco, 1851** (detail)
*Half plate daguerreotype*
*Collection of the Oakland Museum of California,*
*gift of Mr. and Mrs. Willard M. Nott and Dr. Paul S. Taylor by exchange*

Many more finds eventually arrived, but the most rewarding for its rich documentary history, sense of adventure, and notable descriptions of the gold rush was the trove of works donated by Elizabeth Brownell, Isaac Wallace Baker's great-granddaughter. We presently lack details of Baker's life in the Atlantic coastal town of Beverly, Massachusetts, halfway between Gloucester and Marblehead, but we do know that he was a family man and jack-of-all-trades, later showing some talent as an illustrator. He left Beverly to become a sometime adventurer, miner, and daguerreotypist, and after he returned from California's diggings he became a popular lecturer at home and occasionally in Boston.

Far too often photographs are treated as examples of art without the history, provenance, and background that give them much of the meaning that would inform the viewer and return the object to the intent of its making. The Baker collection possesses a singular benefit that goes beyond the usual attributes of daguerreotypes: we have Baker's written account of his adventures as well as the images, in several media — daguerreotype, watercolor, painting, and journal sketch. Each is unique, singular, precious, fragile, yet still well preserved. Together they provide a way to explore along with Baker as he goes about the miner's grueling work and later makes the daguerreotypist's detailed record. Even more surprising, we come to realize that Isaac Wallace Baker well understood his place in history. He had the wide-ranging abilities and talents needed to survive in the free-for-all society of California's raw new frontier cities and gold camps. He easily learned the daguerreotype process and enjoyed a fine sense of delight in the adventurous life he had chosen.

Many private collectors have known about Baker's daguerreotypes, but the broad public rediscovery of cased images as brilliant and valued objects was hardly predictable. Daguerreotypes like Baker's have a new modern importance, which may result in part from recent scholarship and well-illustrated publications about the history of photography. But it is also intriguing to consider the unique place of electronic media in all of this contemporary interest, since nowhere in photography does there exist so comparable an affinity as that between the daguerreotype and the ambience of a computer screen. The screen offers virtually an exact modern translation of a daguerreotype image via the World Wide Web and the Internet, and reproduces it at the scale of 1 : 1. We see that the screen's image retains the daguerreotype's silvery appearance and color, while avoiding the problems of handling and controlling the lighting. These links of new technology to an early, now archaic method of making photographs help us to see daguerreotypes as accessible, contemporary, and compelling.

Perhaps a combination of all these factors made daguerreotypes a model for American photographers of the twentieth century. Walker Evans, for instance, made photographs that often achieve the seemingly humble and ordinary qualities of the daguerreotype. They avoid the look of art and produce a vernacular style important to American photography. Not surprisingly, Evans owned a daguerreotype camera, sought out early images, and became fascinated more by the "look" of these pictures than by the subjects they illustrated.

Recent ideas about photography help us to see that beyond the canon of masters and masterpieces lies a large number of photographs that need not be art or document but are essential to an informed understanding of photography. For example, photographers, however straightforwardly they may think they approach their subject, reveal an attitude: the way the subject is seen discloses the photographer's viewpoint, and the photographer's bias may emerge in subtle ways. Baker understood that the moment of making the picture depended on available light, that it was an important event — possibly formal — but also that it needed accurate, carefully considered, sophisticated props. In Baker's *Native Californian* portrait, a young individual is presented in a respectful manner (pl. 51). We recognize that he is seated properly and holds himself upright, an indication of what Baker had communicated to him and also of what impression he wanted the image to convey. Similarly, the image *Chinese Man* calls attention to the subject's upright pose and centers attention on his braid, an ethnic attribute of the era (pl. 39). Again Baker's attitude is respectful. In this collection, his point of view is given context by the extraordinary written material in the many-volume diary that he kept. The stories, the lectures he later gave, the drawings and paintings, all confirm his largely positive vision.

Baker kept a journal during his California years. He started it on the trip that began on August 13, 1849, in Beverly, on board the barque *San Francisco*, and continued it in California from January 18, 1850, on. In this part of the journal, he made rough but engaging illustrations, as he did again two years later (having gone home briefly in 1851) on his second trip west, aboard the *John Q. Adams*, out of Boston to San Francisco, May 8 to October 20, 1852 — some 150 days at sea. From the journal we learn Baker's first impressions of California. The large-scale paintings that he made after his two trips also have a kind of authority as eyewitness accounts. He completed these works in Beverly as illustrations to accompany his always popular lectures. To understand the kind of journal that Baker kept, we need only read his descriptions of San Francisco, which provide a lively introduction: "'A beautiful country, romantic scenery, excellent harbor, a fine climate and plenty of game — this is the place for *me*,' thinks I, upon sighting land." But he shortly made another judgment:

> "It is the most degraded, immoral, uncivilized and dirty place that can be imagined, and the sooner we are away from *here* the better for us" — were my afterthoughts five minutes after being on the shore. . . . After a long pull from the vessel against a very heavy tide, and passing vessels of all descriptions and of every nation — English, French, Hamburg, Danes, Swedes, Norwegians and Russians as well as Yankees — some ashore; aground, sunk or capsized — some hauled up, stripped and with notices attached, such as "storage," "Lumber for Sale," "boarding and Lodging."[1]

After this reversal of opinion, Baker adds that there was a miniature forest of masts, and "now, what it [San Francisco] formerly has been, what it was only one year since, we all know and (as with every other new country) what it eventually will be still remain to be proved."[2] In his journal, as in his later daguerreotypes, he proves a close observer, thoughtful as well as shrewd, and ready for adventure.

Baker followed the path to the goldfields and experienced the same anticipation, backbreaking labor, and disappointment that most miners did, and thus his descriptions match and enliven our understanding. In the Oakland Museum collection is a splendid plate, *The Levee at Marysville, Yuba County*, by an unknown maker (pl. 25). It helps us to visualize Baker's amusing account of the following encounter on the same levee:

> At the foot of a large oak on the "levee" at the Steamboat landing, we concluded to pitch our tent for a while, as we had a little *trading* to do prior to any mining expedition. Having

*George Henry Burgess (1830–1905)*
**San Francisco in July 1849** (detail), 1891
*Oil on canvas*
*Collection of the Oakland Museum of California, gift of the Women's Board*
*Artist's view of San Francisco at the time of Baker's arrival in 1850.*

done this and regaled ourselves on a little fresh beef, we turned in, tired, with the prospect of a good Sunday rest after a toilsome weeks work. Sunday passed, steamers arrived, and we found ourselves rather in the way, and the next morning I was accosted by a respectable-looking man, dressed in "long togs" and "specs," who very civilly asked me if that was my tent. Thinking he might be a merchant in search of goods and being anxious to "sell cargo," I promptly answered in the affirmative, when he politely informed me that the City authorities didn't allow any tents on the levee, and that I must leave before night.[3]

Baker's account of this stir and action, as reflected in the Oakland Museum daguerreotype, is reunited with its context as part of an inquiry into the pictorial history of the gold rush.

*Isaac Wallace Baker (1810–1862)*
**Miners and Cabin**
*Half plate daguerreotype*
*Collection of the Oakland Museum of California,*
*gift of anonymous donor*

There are journal descriptions as well for Baker's several gold mining daguerreotypes. For example, on the day that he built his cabin, he explains: "There I dug into the hill, levelled a spot, *built* a house and moved into it with my effects in *one day*, and the next, as I was alone, commenced 'prospecting.'"[4] That day he was rewarded, he tells us, with seventy dollars' worth of gold.

But the discovery of such small amounts of gold was not enough. He returned home to Beverly on September 7, 1851, aboard the *Belgrade,* out of Cherryfield, Maine, but soon returned to California to continue the adventure — now as a daguerreotypist associated with Perez M. Batchelder, who was already working in the area of Murphy's Camp, a place that Baker knew well.[5] Although Batchelder and his brothers ran several daguerreian wagons,

Baker's was known for brisk business. The fine quarter plate tells its own story (pl. 48): a wagon fills the frame, yet we can see men seated at the side, as well as the important sign inviting customers to "walk in and examine specimens." This wheeled wagon, like that of William Shew, was ideal for moving among mining camps in search of customers, and in the fire-prone towns of the early West, it provided a swifter means to avoid destruction than being afoot did. More than a documentary record, this image lets us see the spirit of adventure and joy of the proprietor as he stands on the steps.[6]

When Ike Baker, as he was called, in his role as lecturer described "his" California, he highlighted for the audience its awe-inspiring aspects, like the Big Trees just fifteen miles from Murphy's Camp. He depended on the pictured image, unrolling his oversized oil painting of the Sequoia with Indians sitting nearby. It is titled *A Visit from Native Californians*. Baker made the tree credible to his audience, the episodes note, by unrolling a length of linen string that he had wound around the stump, evidence of its circumference, reminding us that he was an educator skilled enough to understand that seeing is believing. Clearly the paintings made the journal visual, as he is reported to have explained in a conversation with his daughter, who wanted him to do yet another painting.[7] For Lizzie, as he called her, he made trips to the shed to pull out watercolors that he taught her to use as well as "daguerreotype parapenalia [*sic*]."[8]

The family wanted Isaac to continue his painting and daguerreotype work at home in Beverly, but as early as 1851 more news of gold arrived, this time in Victoria, Australia. The event soon precipitated another gold rush, to the Southern Hemisphere, and once more the call of adventure claimed Baker. In 1856 he again headed for the goldfields and whatever promise he envisioned there. His family never saw him again; they later got word that he had died in Sumatra.

Baker the photographer left us the rare treasure of his daguerreotypes of Murphy's Camp, Indians, Chinese, and mining views, the signs of commerce, portraits, paintings, and illustrations. In the delightful ambrotype of a poker game, he also left us a legacy of humor (pl. 91). The scene is set up as the game we all want to be in — these players (Baker himself on the left) hold a royal flush and a straight flush. The cards are there for all to see, plainly pictured at the great moment of excitement when the royal flush will overtake the unsuspecting player holding what is usually a winning hand.

Photographs can communicate what was to be seen in California's gold country, but more than that, they inform us of daily details in a manner that convinces us that these goings-on, in this faraway place, were worth the enormous expense and trouble of a daguerreotype setup. The customers wanted their lives and fates recorded, and for most daguerreotypists, this was a once-in-a-lifetime opportunity.

Though even now it seems an unlikely coincidence, the 1850s were not only the decade of the gold rush but also the time when photographic technology became sufficiently well developed to record a moment in time, a face, or an event for anyone who had a few dollars.

*Isaac Wallace Baker*
**Untitled (California Indians), c. 1852**
*Oil painting*
*Collection of the Bancroft Library*

This remarkable intersection of history and art brought a unique event under the scrutiny of a new way of seeing and recording. One hundred fifty years later, we have just begun to explore the effects of this conjunction. In exhibitions and books such as this one, we may be able to perceive the ways in which history and new technology informed and affected each other.

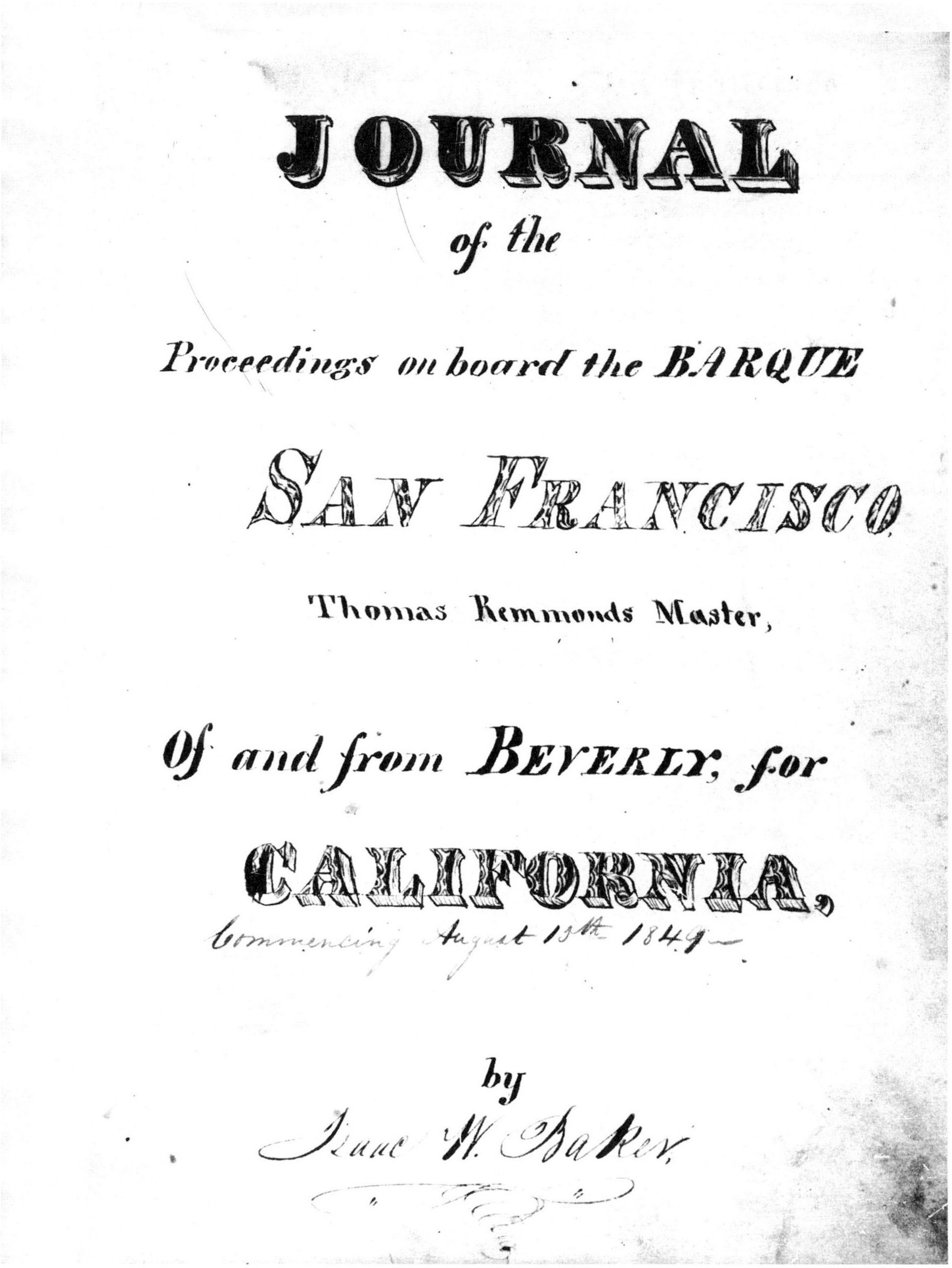

# JOURNAL

### of the

### Proceedings on board the BARQUE

# SAN FRANCISCO

### Thomas Kemmonds Master,

### Of and from BEVERLY, for

# CALIFORNIA,

*Commencing August 13th 1849*

### by

*Isaac W. Baker,*

*Isaac Wallace Baker*
**Cover page of Journal, 1849**
*Collection of the Bancroft Library*

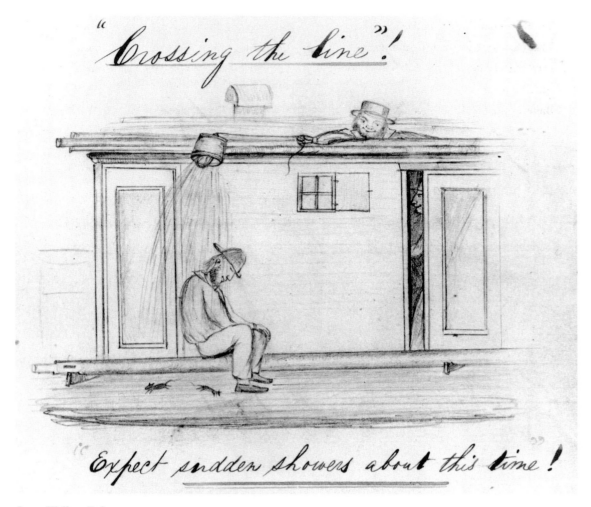

*Isaac Wallace Baker*
**"Crossing the Line!"** (illustration from journal), 1849
*Collection of the Bancroft Library*

### NOTES

1   From Baker's journal (1850), 1; text transcribed from the handwritten original to a typed text produced by Frederick Baker, a grandson. This copy was kept by a great-granddaughter, Elizabeth Brownell, who graciously shared it with the author. Frederick Baker, an engineer who taught at the University of California, also typed the journal copy given to the Oakland Museum with the seven daguerreotypes and one ambrotype. A project for the future would be to check the typed copy against Baker's barely legible handwritten journal in the Bancroft Library, as underlining and other punctuation may not be exactly transcribed.

2   Ibid., 3.

3   Ibid., 26.

4   Ibid., 36.

5   From a map included in the journal, there is an indication that the wagon was at one time situated between Vallecito and Murphy's Camp, on the east side of the road.

6   Therese Thau Heyman, *Mirror of California: Daguerreotypes* (Oakland: Oakland Museum, 1973), 8. There is little secure information, but family tradition suggests the identity of the man.

7   Frederick Baker, "The Bakery," episode 8, 1854; and "Isaac Baker, Jack-of-All-Trades," unpaginated typescript, 13.

8   Baker, "Isaac Baker," 22.

# Acknowledgments

A book of this nature, featuring so many rare historical images, is not possible without the help, support, and generosity of numerous individuals and institutions. Our guest authors, Peter E. Palmquist and John Wood, have graced these pages with their knowledge and passion for their subject. We look to our preface author, Therese Thau Heyman, as our mentor for her early work in collecting daguerreotypes at the Oakland Museum of California, and we thank her for her support throughout the publication and exhibition of our work in this area.

Key to the success of our publication was the gracious assistance received from numerous museums, libraries, and historical agencies throughout the United States. Two local institutions deserve special thanks. At the Bancroft Library, University of California, Berkeley, Bill Roberts, archivist and then acting curator of photography, allowed us extensive use of the library's remarkable archive. At the Society of California Pioneers, San Francisco, Herb Garcia, administrator, Susan Haas, registrar, and Bill McMorris, photography archivist, gladly opened the door to their extraordinary collection. In all of California, no richer or more comprehensive holdings of gold rush images exist than in these two very fine institutions.

Many other institutions and professionals have helped to create this book: Barbara McCandless, associate curator of photographs at the Amon Carter Museum; Emily Wolfe and Robert MacKimmie at the California Historical Society; Gary F. Kurutz, principal librarian, California State Library Special Collections Branch; Therese Mulligan, curator of photography, and James A. Conlin, registrar, International Museum of Photography at George Eastman House; Pierre Apraxine, curator, and Maria Umali, Gilman Paper Company Collection; Cynthia Read-Miller, curator of photography, Henry Ford Museum and Greenfield Village; Jennifer Watts, curator of historical photographs, the Huntington Library; Weston J. Naef, curator of photography, and Jacklyn Burns, Photo Services, the J. Paul Getty Museum; Maria Morris Hambourg, curator in charge, Laura Muir, and Suzanne L. Shenton, the Metropolitan Museum of Art; Bonnie Wilson, curator, sound and visual collections, and Cindy Stimmler, Minnesota Historical Society; Anne E. Havinga, assistant curator, prints, drawings, and photographs, Museum of Fine Arts Boston; National Museum of American History; Tom Sitton, Natural History Museum of Los Angeles County; Mary Wiley, associate director, Newberry Library; Taylor Horton, San Francisco Maritime National Historical Park; Michael Hendrix, director, Siskiyou County Museum; Kim Walters, library director, Braun Research Library, Southwest Museum; Mary Lou Lentz, registrar, Sutter's Fort (State of California, Department of Parks and Recreation); Kathleen Howe, curator of prints and photographs, and Kittu Longstreth-Brown, registrar, the University of New Mexico, University Art Museum; Marianne Babal, Beverley K. Smith, assistant vice president and manager, Bob Chandler, and Bill Sander, Wells Fargo History Department.

It is essential that we acknowledge the help received from the members of the Daguerreian Society and its president, Mark Johnson. Through an advertisement in the society's newsletter we were able to uncover many new cased images. Numerous members of the society are represented in the list of private collectors who have contributed to this publication. We are particularly indebted to them for their generosity in responding to our requests and allowing us to publish their views. Their collections of ambrotypes and daguerreotypes greatly enrich this book. We thank each of them: Stephen Anaya, Mrs. Vivienne Bekeart, Stanley B. Burns, M.D., R. Bruce Duncan, Gary Ewer, Greg French, Matthew R. Isenburg, Marc and Mona Klarman, W. Bruce Lundberg, John McWilliams, Carl Mautz, Joan Murray, Peter E. Palmquist, Graham Pilecki, Charles Schwartz, Robert Harshorn Shimshak, Joseph T. Silva, Leonard A. Walle, Dennis Waters, and the family of Helen Weber Kennedy, especially Peggy Cahill.

We are indebted to numerous colleagues at the Oakland Museum of California who contributed to the exhibition and catalog. Cherie Newell edited the manuscript for us and provided perceptive advice and moral support throughout the project. Registrars Joy Tahan and Janice Capecci and preparators Kaoru Kitagawa, Deborah Lohrke, and Mark Perko showed a genuine enthusiasm for the images and for solving the knotty problem of their display. Carl Ryanen-Grant and Gabriel Cothes provided research on many of the images. Our director, Dr. Dennis Power, immediately understood the value of cased images in interpreting the Gold Rush. L. Thomas Frye, Carey Caldwell, Phil Linhares, Valerie Verzuh, Kathy Borgogno, Diane Curry, and Claudia Kishler assisted in ways too numerous to mention.

A special thanks goes to John S. Hartz and the staff of Camera Corner, Oakland, for generously donating copy photography. Their cheerful attitudes and enthusiasm for the images reminded us of the uniqueness of each image. Thanks are also due Rudy Ruzicska, who so graciously provided us with beautiful color transparencies; Robert Hartman, who provided early inspiration; and our spouses, Amy Williams and Steve Chaikin.

# Introduction

*Marcia Eymann*

All of us do it. We pick up a camera and look through the lens to take a photograph. It's simple. It's commonplace. Have you ever noticed, as you look through the lens, that your perspective of the scene has changed? You see the subject from a new and different angle. Ask any photographer and he or she will tell you the view is different, that there is a unique perspective through the eye of the camera. A simple photograph tells a compelling, evocative story, captured with the click of the shutter, freezing a moment in time.

When gold was discovered in 1848 at Sutter's Mill, photography was not yet a decade old. In that short period of time, in the form of the daguerreotype, the new technique had grown in popularity and become an integral part of the American way of life. Numerous unrelated daguerreian photographers, practicing their art independently, have left us an incredible visual legacy that tells the story of the argonauts who ventured to California by land or by sea to seek their fortunes. These images graphically depict the individuals, the growth of a state, and the legacy of the gold rush to the people and landscape of America. They allow you and me to look directly into the faces of the men and women who chose to make the journey — and to see how it changed them forever.

In the pages that follow we invite you to walk in the footsteps of the forty-niners to see what the California gold rush looked like. The three essays here explore different perspectives on gold rush photography. Drew Johnson, in "Mementos of Silver and Gold: California and the 'True Reflected Likeness,'" discusses the personal significance of the daguerreian image to nineteenth-century Americans, especially to the forty-niners and their families. In "Theatrical Narratives and the Documents of Dream: California and the Great American Image," John Wood reveals the daguerreian image as an icon that created a heroic figure on a grand adventure to change his lot in life and explains why such an event is not likely to happen again. In "The Sad but True Story of a Daguerreian Holy Grail," Peter E. Palmquist focuses on the legendary tale of the lost three-hundred-plate daguerreotype panorama of California by Robert H. Vance.

Today we interpret history partly from the photographers' point of view. We use their visual interpretations to examine changes in landscape, costume, the development of communities, and the individuals, great and small, who shaped history. Through photography, in the form of the daguerreotype and ambrotype, this publication and the related exhibition will visually tell the story of the California gold rush, the first major world event to be documented photographically.

Our odyssey begins with a look at the faces of the individuals who populated California before the world rushed in. The young Indian boy by Isaac Wallace Baker (pl. 51) and *Nisenan Indian Man with Arrows* (pl. 1) represent the inhabitants of the foothills region of the Sierra Nevada mountain range. Their land, and their lives, would be forever changed by the invasion of gold seekers. Immigrants from Spain and Mexico, called Californios, began arriving in 1769 and remained to prosper in an agrarian society. In the portraits of Andreas Pico (pl. 53) and María Rosalia Vallejo Leese, sister to wealthy landowner Mariano Vallejo (pl. 54), we see individuals who are well established in the region. One a military man, the other a member of a prominent and influential family — both are people of wealth and power, as their clothing and their aristocratic bearing indicate.

Throughout the late 1830s and 1840s Americans immigrated to California, then a Mexican territory. These Americans married into Californio families and established themselves as landowners, often becoming Mexican citizens. It is difficult to discuss the prediscovery period without including a portrait of Captain John Sutter, the man who, before the gold rush, was one of the wealthiest landowners in the territory (pl. 55). Upon relinquishing his American citizenship, Sutter was awarded by the Mexican territorial governor the largest possible land grant, 48,400 acres, at the junction of the Sacramento and American Rivers. Following the discovery of gold on his land, Sutter's own workmen deserted him, and his vast rancho was taken over by squatters, who despoiled his property. By 1852, just four years after gold was discovered, he was bankrupt, destined to live out his life an impoverished man.

News of the discovery of gold at Sutter's Mill on January 24, 1848, did not spread quickly by modern standards. Because of the scarcity and slowness of communication, as well as general skepticism, it took two or three months for a real rush to develop. By May rumors of gold were running rampant throughout the California territory. On May 12, San Francisco newspaperman and promoter Sam Brannan took to the streets of the city, carrying a bottle of gold flakes in his hand and shouting, "Gold! Gold! Gold from the American River!" Following this dramatic announcement, word of the discovery spread like wildfire across the country and around the world. In words of the time: "The whole country, from San Francisco to Los Angeles, and from the sea shore to the base of the Sierra Nevadas, resounds with the sordid cry of '*gold*, GOLD, GOLD!' while the field is left half planted, the house half built, and everything neglected but the manufacture of shovels and pickaxes." [1]

A motto commonly used by photographers at the time of the gold discovery, "Secure the shadow 'ere the substance fade,/Let Nature imitate what Nature made!" promoted their work and encouraged clients to take advantage of their art. With the rush for gold reaching a fevered pace, the motto took on new meaning for the adventurers who set their sights on California. "Nobody who travels knows that he shall return," stated a clipping of 1848. "Therefore he ought to leave something behind for his friends to remember him by. What can be more appropriate than a Daguerreotype? because nothing can represent the features so well and so accurately." [2] Such a comment is typical of daguerreotypists' frank appeal to the sentiments of their potential clientele. Don't go to the goldfields without leaving some of yourself behind. After all, you might not return! For George W. Northrup of Minnesota, the line might better read, "You might never leave." After having his portrait taken in full forty-niner gear, Northrup stayed in his adopted home state of Minnesota and never left for the goldfields (pl. 58). Instead he established himself as a seasoned frontiersman and was sought after for his skills as an experienced wilderness guide. During the Civil War, he joined the U.S. cavalry and died in the line of duty fighting the Sioux in the Battle of Killdeer Mountain, on July 28, 1864.

In a portrait taken by Henry Insley of New York, we have the unique opportunity to see an argonaut, Charles B. Curtiss, before he leaves New York for California in 1849 and again after he arrives at his destination (pls. 59 and 60). Curtiss's cleanly shaved face and unsullied clothing in the second portrait lead us to believe that this image was taken before he actually began mining. These two portraits demonstrate the changes in clothing and demeanor that occurred in a man from the time of his first learning of the discovery of gold to his arrival in California and show how he prepared himself to become a miner. In the later image he is no longer dressed in a suit and tie but has taken on the costume of the forty-niner, prepared to meet the elements and his destiny.

More self-documentation of miners is seen in the portrait of E. Deane (pl. 63) and *Young Forty-Niner with Rifle and Shovel* (pl. 61). These images depict innocence in the faces of idealistic young men. Take a moment to study their faces, their hair, eyes, clothes, and stance. These are men ready to embark on a great adventure, to leave home, to risk their lives, make their fortune, and stare danger and death straight in the eye.

Of course, to accomplish their goal they first had to make their way to California. They had two basic options, both plagued by hardships and filled with the mystery of the unknown. From April 1849 through April 1850, 62,000 would-be miners landed in San Francisco's harbor. Their long journey by ship from some Eastern port such as Boston (pl. 64), around turbulent Cape Horn, stopping briefly in Valparaiso, Chile (pl. 66), thence northward through the Pacific to San Francisco, might take an average of four to eight months, depending on weather conditions. Though viewed as relatively safe, the long sea journey was actually fraught with hazards and took its toll on passengers. Conditions aboard ship were seldom as advertised. Cramped quarters, bad food, and months of inactivity often brought the argonauts to San Francisco in poor physical condition, unprepared for the rigors of prospecting for gold.

The other choice was the torturous overland trek. This route took the argonauts across the Great Plains and the Rocky Mountains, through the heart of America, allowing them to see the country and experience the dangers and difficulties of cross-country travel, mainly on foot. In 1849, 32,000 people, most of them young men in their twenties and thirties, made the difficult journey, battling harsh weather conditions, inadequate food, water, and medical treatment, and numerous other hardships. For many of them it was a series of firsts. The first time away from home. The first time to sail on a steamboat (pl. 69), sleep on the ground, hold a gun, or encounter a Native American (pl. 71). This rugged, strenuous, and oftentimes fatal trip might last as long as eight months before they reached the goldfields of California at last.

During their journeys and upon arrival, the forty-niners bore constant witness to history. Today, through the rich treasure of the photographic record, we can share their experience. Like the forty-niners, we arrive at the bustling port of San Francisco and take note of a city that has tripled in size since the discovery of gold (pl. 4). One needs only to compare the panoramas of 1851 (pl. 6) and 1853 (pl. 34) to see the dramatic changes.

Stroll down the streets of San Francisco (pl. 130) and Sacramento (pl. 112) or examine the details of a miners' tent store, with its numerous goods on display (pl. 109). Best of all, see how the miners lived and plied their newfound trade. In *Mining Scene at Grizzly Flat, Placer County*, the morning dew is actually visible, giving the image an almost fairy-tale quality (pl. 15). The miners who lived here seem to have chosen a magical location to seek their fortune. Other views show the miners in a multicultural atmosphere (pl. 76). Still others document the advance in technology with industrialized and hydraulic mining, for example *Miners Working Under Sluice Network* (pl. 28) and *Hydraulic Mining, Placerville, El Dorado County* (pl. 119).

We have the opportunity to catch a glimpse of the miners' living conditions in *Group of Miners in Front of a Barracks* (pl. 90) and *"An Evening Scene, Boston Flat, Calveras County"* (*Miner Playing the Flute by his Cabin*) (pl. 11). We see the ruggedness of their homes, their isolation and loneliness. They are real men, at work and at play (pl. 91), in happiness and in sorrow, in life and in death (pl. 32).

Perhaps the most significant aspect of these California images is the faces that look back at us, and what they can tell us 150 years later. In the portrait of *Sarah Anne MacDougal with Elizabeth*, we see more than just a likeness (pl. 75). The label found inside this cased image states, "This is Sarah MacDougal and her daughter upon her arrival in California, January, 1850." Look closely at her hairline, hands, and wrists. You will see evidence of sunburn, probably suffered on her cross-country journey. Women of that time avoided exposure to the sun and kept themselves covered, but on such a long journey that was not possible. Thanks to the detail of the camera, evidence of Sarah's sunburn provides us with insight that helps us to better understand nineteenth-century life.

In another daguerreian portrait, we see a different type of woman looking out at us. Eliza Steen Johnson was a young Irish woman who in 1843, at the age of nineteen, eloped with John Johnson from Oldstone, Ireland. They arrived early in California's gold rush, to make their fortune not in mining but in retail. Eliza and her husband ran the Lace House on Sacramento Street just off Portsmouth Square in San Francisco. In a community that was sorely short on women, imagine the miners' delight in seeing this lively and lovely young woman model clothing for them as they brought in their pokes filled with gold dust to purchase gifts for loved ones back home. Even in this early 1850s portrait, Eliza, the successful merchant, is

*Unknown maker*
**Eliza Jane Steen Johnson**
*Sixth plate daguerreotype*
*Collection of the Oakland Museum of California,*
*gift of Barbara Smith*

*Charles Christian Nahl*
**Portrait of Eliza Jane Steen Johnson, 1858**
*Oil on canvas*
*34¼ × 26½ in.*
*Collection of the Oakland Musuem of California,*
*gift of Dr. Gerald H. Gray*

*A. Findlay*
**A Sunday, Forbestown, July 18, 1869**
*Oil painting*
*Collection of the Oakland Museum of California,*
*gift of Mr. and Mrs. Rollen Gaskill*

dressed in the height of fashion and adorned with jewelry. Compare this with the painting of her done in 1858 by Charles Christian Nahl and notice the differences in the two images. The painting portrays a dignified and wealthy woman, calm and composed. In contrast, the daguerreotype shows us the *real* Eliza Steen Johnson — a living and breathing woman who looks squarely out at you with unflinching certainty from under the protective glass of the daguerreian case.

Reaching the end of our pictorial account of the gold rush, we find the photographers themselves, documenting their own presence. In the daguerreotype *Baker in Front of Batchelder's Daguerrian Saloon*, we see Isaac Wallace Baker outside his itinerant studio somewhere in the goldfields, ready to greet customers (pl. 48). William Shew's *Daguerreian Saloon* in San Francisco shows the artist's studio in a prominent location next to the *Alta California* newspaper office (pl. 149). Here, we gain greater insight into the working environment of these photographic pioneers, who have taken us back in time through their reflected images of the past.

The eye of the camera is as unique as the eye of the beholder, and the discovery of photography carried an impact that affected the entire world. This is as true today as in photography's infancy. Early photographers refined their art, pushing it to new limits. Their point of

*Unknown maker*
**View of Forbestown, Butte County**
*Half plate ambrotype*
*Collection of Joseph T. Silva*

view changed the way the past would be perceived by future generations. Knowingly or un-knowingly, these artists created a visual documentation of history as it happened. Through their eyes, and the eye of the camera, their visual perspective of the world has transcended time, providing us with dynamic and beautiful images of California as it was before, during, and after the world rushed in. The eye of the camera brought about dramatic change — change that we can not only talk about but also see with our own eyes, hold in our hands, and fiercely believe in.

So come, join us in returning visually to the days of legend and to the land of adventure, danger, sin, wealth, ruin, and, above all, GOLD!

**NOTES**

1   Edward C. Kemble, "The History of California Newspapers," *Sacramento Daily Union*, December 25, 1848, in Rodman W. Paul, *California Gold: The Beginning of Mining in the Far West* (Lincoln: University of Nebraska Press, 1947), 19.

2   Clipping dated March 4, 1848, Langennheim Archives, American Museum of Photography, Philadelphia, in Beaumont Newhall, *The Daguerreotype in America* (N.p.: Duell, Sloan, and Pearce, 1961), 67.

# Silver & Gold

# Mementos of Silver and Gold

## California and the "True Reflected Likeness"

*Drew Heath Johnson*

*Where is taught that blest art which keeps the absent near[?]*

*Remember that your letters, your daguerreotype and my tears are all the consolation I can have.*

A daguerreotype is a private object. In the late twentieth-century world of art museums and full-color exhibition catalogs devoted to nineteenth-century photography, it is sometimes easy to overlook this fundamental quality. Recent years have seen an astounding rebirth of the daguerreotype, with a profusion of books and prestigious exhibitions celebrating the first photographs. It is no longer unusual for individual daguerreotypes, fiercely fought over by eager collectors and institutions, to obtain six-figure prices at posh auction houses.

Considering the unique physical beauty and historic appeal of daguerreotypes, this is all quite understandable, even past due. Such public recognition does, however, tend to divert attention from the essentially humble origins of cased images. Commissioned for personal reasons by the sitters themselves, daguerreotypes and ambrotypes were meant to be appreciated individually, held in the hand by those intimately connected with the subject portrayed. For the most part, daguerreotypes were reflected upon, quietly and in private. That is why opening a daguerreotype case today always carries with it a slight sense of prying, of intruding upon an object of intimacy and sentiment.

This is especially true with images of the California gold rush, for the complex of personal motivations behind the creation of cased images was influenced by powerful and unique social forces. Here daguerreotypes carried a singular power bolstered by the anxiety of separation across vast physical distances. For those involved in the great rush for Western gold, daguerreotypes helped to fill the emotional void created by separation as no other object could. Along with letters, the new art of photography was the most important way in which a forty-niner and his family could honor the bonds of family and affection, on occasion even transcending mortality itself. Nothing else can explain the desperate eagerness of forty-niners and their families to obtain photographic likenesses.

On that legendary January morning in 1848 when James Marshall stooped to examine the flakes of shiny metal that lay in the tailrace of the California sawmill that belonged to his boss, John Sutter, photography in America was less than a decade old. Inventor Louis-Jacques-Mandé Daguerre had presented his ingenious and beautiful method for preserving the image formed in the camera obscura to the French Academy of Sciences in August 1839. Purchased from the inventor by the French government, Daguerre's process was given to the world without patent restrictions, a circumstance that guaranteed its swift journey to American shores.

In the years before Marshall's fateful discovery, the daguerreotype had assumed a prominent place in American culture. Almost overnight, scores of Yankee tinkerers had duplicated Daguerre's invention, in the process establishing a burgeoning photographic industry to supply a seemingly insatiable demand for portraits and views. Horace Greeley's famous observation that "in daguerreotypes we beat the world" was not just a hollow boast. American artists quickly established technical superiority in image-making, winning the highest prizes at international fairs and causing envious European daguerreotypists to boast that they possessed knowledge of "the American Process." Even Ralph Waldo Emerson was moved to quip, " 'Tis certain that the Daguerreotype is the true Republican style of painting. The artist stands aside and lets you paint yourself." [1]

Such twentieth-century historians of photography as Beaumont Newhall, Richard Rudisill, and John Wood have expertly revealed the blend of social, cultural, and aesthetic forces that drove Americans from all classes to embrace the new art, in the process transforming photography into a fixture of American life.[2] The broad scope of daguerreian practice and photography's pervasive everyday presence in the lives of Americans are difficult to overstate. Responding to the "exuberant nationalism" of antebellum life, daguerreotypists produced images that attempted to reveal the American character in terms of national ideals. The affordability of daguerreotypes, their striking detail, and their associative power all combined, in Wood's felicitous phrase, to "render the mundane heroic" in thousands of portraits of ordinary Americans. "The daguerreotypists, without ever actually framing such a question, obviously did ask: how can I make my sitter look heroic; how can I imbue this visage with hope, promise, and a strength reminiscent of the classical?"[3]

If Eastern states responded enthusiastically to the daguerreotype, distant California, in the midst of its lunatic rush for mineral wealth, provided an even richer climate for photography. The California experience, a shared process of mass emigration from the East, risk, and hardship, created a voracious hunger for photographic images. Here, the daguerreotype's function as private memento and personal relic achieved its greatest power. Created, like most daguerreotypes, on an individual basis for strictly private purposes, cased photographic images became the treasured means by which the world established a personal connection to the gold rush.

Forty-niners were essentially aliens in a strange land, separated by months of travel from friends and family. The majority of miners considered themselves, and were in fact, transient, intending to stay just long enough to make their fortunes and then return home. Despite the high hopes and expectations, the boisterous humor and the sense of adventure, the gold rush experience was laced with an undercurrent of menace and despair. Even for those few miners who struck it rich, California could seem a place of dislocation, loneliness, and brutal labor. "Suicides caused by disappointment," wrote one miner, "are as numerous as the deaths resulting from natural causes." All found the California experience difficult; a few could see nothing beyond their own bitterness. "A residence here at present," wrote one argonaut, "is a pilgrimage in a strange land, a banishment from good society, a living death, and a punish-

*Unknown maker*
**Lyman Alvinson Rundell in His Miner's Frock**
*Sixth plate daguerreotype*
*Collection of John McWilliams*

ment of the worst kind, and the time spent here ought to be considered as a blank period in existence, and accordingly struck from the record of one's days." [4]

In such an environment, personal objects that recalled home and family acquired rare power. Likely to be regarded with sentiment in the East, in California the new art of photography served to reinforce family ties, preserve the memory of the dead, assert an immigrant's place within his group, and sustain a forty-niner's sense of connection to home. It is this personal, even intimate, side of the gold rush experience that holds the key to the daguerreotype's significance in California. Here, more than anywhere else, the daguerreotype "operated in significant symbolic ways by evoking memory, by preserving sentiment, or by broadening experience beyond one's immediate environment." [5]

Adversities and the pain of separation began with the start of the voyage west, and enterprising daguerreian artists were on hand to document it. Stopping in Buffalo to provision, overland forty-niner William Swain seemed to suggest that a daguerreotype to leave at home was among the standard effects of a miner traveling overland: "I have bought a trunk for $3 with two straps on it. I have priced all the rifles in town and find that I can get one that will answer for about $15 and good revolvers at the same price. I have had my likeness taken and cased for $2 and shall send it to Sabrina . . . with a token of fond remembrance. My coats I have not looked after yet, it being darkish when I got through at the daguerrian rooms." [6] Beginning a round-the-Horn sea voyage to the goldfields, eighteen-year-old Charles Dornin made sure to carry a small library, a journal, his Bible, and his "mother's daguerreotype, over which I cried often and bitterly, when suffering from that most distressing of all heart-diseases, 'home-sickness.' " [7]

After news of the gold discovery, Eastern photographic galleries noticed a conspicuous increase in business, driven by the public's acute desire for personal visual records. "The daguerreotype establishments are overrun with fathers, brothers, cousins," wrote a New York paper, "all getting likenesses to leave to the family they are deserting." [8] Distinguished New York daguerreotypist Abraham Bogardus remembered the period as especially profitable: "On steamer days . . . the gallery would be filled with miners in rough suits carrying their mining tools and a pair of pistols in the belt. We made several sittings before he left the chair and usually sold them all." [9]

Such portraits, besides commemorating the emigrant's historic embarkation on "the great adventure," provided welcome solace for those left behind. The gold rush was an experience intensely shared by those who remained at home. Family members also endured the pain of separation and, through letters and daguerreotypes, glimpsed the incidents and activities of the forty-niners. In Youngstown, New York, Sabrina Swain piercingly described the pain of separation to her absent husband, William: "I want very much to describe my feelings as near as I can, but in doing so I hope not to crucify yours. I feel as though I was alone in the world. The night you left home I did not, nor could not, close my eyes to sleep. Sis [their daughter] slept very well, awoke in the morning, and looked over at me seemingly to welcome a spree with her father, but to her disappointment the looked-for one was absent. She appears very lonesome, and seems to miss you very much. She is very troublesome and will not go to anyone, but cries after me and clings to me more than ever." [10]

Similarly, Fanny Boardman wrote from Sheffield, Massachusetts, to her husband in San Francisco: "I received your letter Saturday evening . . . and that relieved me a good deal although I read it over three times and then cried for an hour, as hard as I could. But my dear it was not at anything in the letter that I cried but because I knew then that you was *really gone*. . . . I slept with it under my head for a week and read it every night before I went to sleep. You may say this was very foolish in me to cry and feel so bad. Perhaps it was. But remember that your letters, your daguerreotype and my tears are all the consolation I can have." [11]

A surviving quarter plate daguerreotype commemorates the beginning of one overland journey (pl. 62). In this remarkable view, Charles W. Cox and Walter Brewster of Battle Creek, Michigan, have pause ' to have a likeness taken of them at the reins of their well-equipped wagon. In the background are seen buildings typical of the hundreds of small towns that miners left behind. A note pinned to the inside of the case explains: "This daguerreotype was taken in March of 1849 at Battle Creek. The Men are Charles W. Cox . . . and Walter Brewster, as they were ready to start overland for the gold diggings in California. They drove these two teams through without serious mishap." [12]

Upon arrival in California, travel-hardened miners found a host of eager daguerreotypists ready to supply portraits. It is not surprising that miners often marked the event with a new daguerreotype portrait, showing them decked out in rough Western clothes, or "California fixin's." As daguerreotypist Henry W. Bradley discovered, "Californians were so anxious that their friends in civilized countries should see just how they looked in their mining dress, with their terrible revolver, the handle protruding menacingly from the holster, somehow, twisted in front, when sitting for a daguerreotype to send to the States! They were proud of their curling moustaches and flowing beards; their bandit-looking *sombreros*." Happily capitalizing on this desire, Bradley boasted to have "accumulated much *oro en polvo* and many yellow coins from . . . private mints." [13]

From the beginning, the gold rush was recognized as a historic event, an adventure of epic proportions. "1849 will ever be a memorable epoch in the history of our country," wrote an overland traveler from Michigan. "Neither the Crusades nor Alexander's expedition to India (all things considered) can equal this emigration to California." [14] Gold seekers were commonly referred to as "argonauts," and their journey as an "odyssey," terms that reinforced the mythic nature of the California experience. One's participation in such an event was clearly *important*, worthy of observance and deliberate commemoration. Gold rush California, in the words of Kevin Starr, "was a society so new that one's very presence in it had historical overtones; everyone had a chance to make history." [15] Like the countless surviving diaries of miners, photographs served as a way to record and preserve one's participation in the making of that history.

Home ties were never more strongly felt in California than at the arrival of mail from "the states." The commotion generated on "Steamer Day" became legendary in San Francisco.

*Unknown maker*
**Miner with Tousled Hair and Swollen Hands**
*Sixth plate daguerreotype*
*Collection of W. Bruce Lundberg*

"The arrival of a steamer with a mail ran the usual excitement and activity of the town up to its highest possible notch," noted journalist Bayard Taylor. "The little Post Office, half-way up the hill, was almost hidden from sight by the crowds that clustered around it. Mr. Moore, the new Postmaster . . . barred every door and window from the moment of his entrance and, with his sons and a few clerks, worked steadily for two days and two nights till the distribution of twenty thousand letters was completed." [16]

In a society of immigrants, news from home was more than a pleasant diversion — it was of vital importance to a miner's emotional well-being. Homesickness was universal among the forty-niners. For such men and their families back home, the art of letter writing quickly became "a dynamic process by which the entire nation was emotionally involved in the rush to California." [17] That a daguerreotype of a distant loved one was among the most prized of objects to receive in mail from home can hardly be doubted. A journalist in remote Humboldt County wrote of the commotion that mail day aroused in even the smaller towns: "RECEIPT OF LETTERS. — It was a source of pleasure to us to witness the expression of satisfaction displayed by a large portion of the crowd which surrounded the Post Office in this place on the day of the arrival of the steamer, awaiting each in 'his turn,' to get news from the loved ones at *home*. Here we saw one with the daguerreotype of a sweetheart; there, another a letter from wife, children and parents. The occurrence would scarcely be noticed in any other portion of the United States, but here it is a primary consideration." [18]

Of course, forty-niners sent portraits back home as well, and California photographers discovered that business became especially brisk whenever a ship was about to leave for the East. As daguerreian Henry Bradley's biographer noted, "The courteous artist was hardly allowed time to breathe, much less to eat, or take a moment's rest or two before the departure of the steamer." Photographer William Shew simply advised patrons not to come at such times: "In consequence of the great demand for pictures at this establishment just before the sailing of each steamer, it is impossible to accommodate all that call at that time, therefore it is for your advantage to call soon after the steamer leaves, and you will have a much better chance to get good pictures." [19]

In the highly competitive marketplace of California, shrewd daguerreians skillfully exploited this desire to establish a photographic connection to home. J. Ruth, a traveling daguerreotypist operating out of the St. Charles Hotel in the town of Shasta, humbly offered "an excellent opportunity for young gentlemen to procure a most acceptable present for some loved friend in the East. Perhaps a sister, or a mother, or more likely, some 'bonnie blue-eyed lassie.' Call and examine his pictures any way, and take some female friend with you." [20] Another daguerreian claimed his pictures were a chance for miners "to give their friends in the States an idea of the effect which a rough and tumble life, and a California sky and climate has had upon their personal appearance," adding significantly, " 'Remember the loved ones at home.' " [21]

In this way, distant family milestones were recorded by the camera. Mexican War veteran John William Tudor Gardiner wrote his mother from California with news of a new son: "I

*Unknown maker*
**California Forty-Niner**
*Quarter plate daguerreotype*
*Collection of the Amon Carter Museum*

sent you a daguerreotype of him from Los Angeles. It ought to be received with this." [22] A daguerreotype from Robert Vance's studio in the collection of the Oakland Museum of California tells a familiar story (pl. 101). A note inside the case records the circumstances and motive behind its creation, right down to the cost of its postage east: "James D. Parker, born Jany. 17th, 1820 in New Bedford, Mass. This daguerreotype was taken for him at Weaverville, Trinity County about 400 miles north of San Francisco, California, October 30th 1853, and sent to Jacob Parker his father by the U. States Mail and rec'd by him Dec'm 13th 1853. Postage paid by James 76 cents."

The emotional impact and consoling power of receiving such an image in the mail could be overwhelming. "I received your daguerrean," wrote Sabrina Swain to her husband, William. "I think I never saw anything but life look more natural. I showed it to Little Cub, and to my astonishment and pleasure she appeared to recognize it. She put her finger on it, looked up at me and laughed, put her face down to yours, and kissed it several times in succession. Every time it comes in her sight she will cry after it." [23] In Massachusetts Fanny Boardman received a daguerreian locket from her husband in San Francisco: "I got your letter of May 30 containing a little locket for Frank and one for my own little self which did me worlds of good." Her response illustrates the way in which daguerreotypes could actually become invested with personal characteristics of the sitter: "Our dear little boy is very well and very fleshy, says Papa a great many times a day and has to see your picture and kiss Papa every day. You would feel yourself paid for the money you spent for that locket even if it was no consolation to me, to see the comfort Frank takes in looking at it and kissing it. He throws kisses to you every day." [24] The power of a daguerreotype to assume, by surrogate, the personal attributes of the sitter is indicated by the number of surviving portraits showing individuals posing with a daguerreotype of a distant or departed loved one (pls. 106, 123).

Throughout the first decade of photography, insightful observers commented on the ability of daguerreotypes to somehow reveal or express human truth. "The Daguerreotype possesses the sublime power to transmit the almost living image of our loved ones," claimed a correspondent to the *Photographic and Fine Art Journal*, "to call up their memories vividly to our mind, and to preserve not only the sparkling eye and winning smile, but to catch the living forms and features of those that are so fondly endeared to us, and to hold them indelibly fixed upon the tablet for years after they have passed away." [25] Photography, wrote San Francisco daguerreotypist William Shew, "has a charming and romantic interest, growing out of the many pleasing associations connected with it. . . . This is especially the case with those, like most Californians, far distant from the hallowed associations of early life. . . . The son or brother as he gazes on the true, reflected likeness of a revered parent, now no more, or of a loved sister, whom he has not seen for years . . . blesses the art that can thus immortalize their images." In the transient environment of California, Shew asserted, photography was nothing less than a sacred gift, an art that, "with us all, is consecrated as a tributary to our holiest affections." [26]

*Arthur Burdett Frost*
**Waiting for the Mail, San Francisco Post Office, 1849,** *c. 1890*
*Oil on canvas*
*24 × 31½ in.*
*Collection of the Oakland Museum of California,*
*Kahn Collection*

The ideal of the photographic portrait as a precious object, to be preserved as the sacred memory of an individual, was widely shared in California. In remote Trinity County, photographer Oliver H. P. Norcross spoke reverently of "that blest art which keeps the absent near."[27] Similarly, renowned San Francisco daguerreian Robert Vance waxed poetic in proclaiming his gallery a temple to the associative power of his portraits:

> Here Art, triumphant, our attention claims,
> Here life seems speaking from a hundred frames,
> Men, women, children, throng the pictured walls,
> Each face each form, its living type recalls.
> Features, complexion, attitude, attire,

Beauty's soft smile, and manhood's glance of fire,

Truly reflected from the burnished plate,

Astonish life with its own duplicate.[28]

Understandably, the loss of a photographic portrait was viewed as a serious misfortune. **"Lost,"** advertised a Eurekan, "BETWEEN Eureka and Central Prairie, Eel River, April 9th, a DAGUERREOTYPE LIKENESS of a Lady and two Children. Any person finding the above will be suitably rewarded by leaving it at the office of the HUMBOLDT TIMES, and also confer a lasting obligation upon SAMUEL BALENTINE." When the ship *Northerner* sank off the California coast, a local journalist used the recovery of an ambrotype washed ashore as an opportunity to reflect upon the fragility of life. "The picture was picked up on the beach, near where the steamer was lost. The features are perfect, the face full, large mouth and a stern countenance."[29] In 1854 the editor of *Humphrey's Journal* used a similar incident to remind his fellow daguerreians of the value of their product: "On board of that ill-fated vessel, the San Francisco, was a Daguerreotype — it sunk with the vessel; its owner was saved, and with the warmest anxiety offered a reward of *five thousand dollars* for the recovery of that single impression. This fact is worthy of the consideration of those who are putting off obtaining Daguerreotype likenesses until a more convenient season." What is a daguerreotype? the editor mused. "In our hands it is a mere article of commerce. But how changed when it is received by those for whom it was originally designed; they look upon every feature, and trace in the expression some happy remembrance. The care exhibited in the charge of this memento is marked by a gentleness known and prompted only by pure love or the warmest friendship. No price can rectify the loss."[30]

The physical appearance of daguerreotypes, so striking to modern observers, no doubt contributed to this sense of the precious. Words like "gem," "jewel," and "fairy work" appear frequently in early descriptions of the medium. The effect was no doubt enhanced by the inherent fragility of the daguerreian image and the way in which it was presented to the buying public: tooled-leather cases lined with silk or velvet, gold-like brass mats and clasps, ornate frames. Most important of all was the indefinable quality of the daguerreian image itself, furtive and yet razor-sharp — a quality that could really be appreciated only by holding the daguerreotype in one's hands, resulting in an experience that can best be described as *intimate*.

Added to this was the borderline occultism of photography itself: frighteningly detailed, irrefutably accurate pictures produced, as if by magic, in a darkened room by a "professor" employing secret (al)chemical processes. Although the daguerreotype was widely accepted as a product of advanced technology, the process and its capabilities were poorly grasped, and misunderstandings about the nature of the medium were common. Daguerreotypists were occasionally asked to photograph objects and people not physically present, and for much of the nineteenth century the eyes of murder victims were commonly thought to hold "retinal images" of their assailants, which could be photographed. Popular literature of the time contains numerous references to the mystical or allegorical properties of daguerreotypes.[31]

*Joshua H. Peirce, Charles E. Peregoy*
**San Francisco in 1851**
*Wood engraving, lettersheet with handwriting*
*Collection of the Oakland Museum of California, Museum Donors' Acquisition Fund*
*The forty-niners' desire to include pictorial images with*
*letters led to the popularity of the lettersheet.*

But the most compelling and genuine attribute of daguerreotypes for gold rush Americans was their ability to stop time, to preserve the appearance of people and places, no matter how distant in time or space. The notion that physical distances could be shattered by photography was grasped by observers from the earliest days of the medium. In 1839, the year of Daguerre's announcement, the French writer Jules Janin remarked that the daguerreotype "is not a picture . . . it is the faithful memory of what man has built throughout the world and of landscapes everywhere. . . . You will write to Rome: Send me by post the dome of St. Peter's; and the dome of St. Peter's will come to you by return mail." [32]

Perhaps inevitably, the immediate and captivating emotional appeal of daguerreotypes could assume a pathological or obsessive character, as the sad case of a French immigrant to San Francisco named Maurin suggests. Apparently having fallen on hard times, Maurin had "been loafing about town some time, having no visible means of support. His room was searched . . . and a large number of daguerreotypes, which are known to have been stolen from the galleries in this city, were found." Three days later, under the headline MONO-MANIA, papers reported: "Mous. M. Maurin, who was arrested on Friday for stealing Daguerreotype likenesses, was discharged by the Mayor on Saturday, on the ground of mono-mania. It appears that his wife left him not long ago, since which time every female portrait he sees he imagines to be the likeness of his wife, to which he thinks he has a right. The unfortunate man will be examined as regards his sanity by Judge Freelon."[33] The thief had been remarkably industrious. "A letter was received signed by nearly all the daguerreian artists in town, stating that they had lost pictures, and supposed Maurin to be the man who had taken them."[34] Apparently the man stole the likenesses from gallery displays. The incident provides a rather extreme example of the passionate allure that daguerreotypes could hold for a dislocated and disappointed immigrant. In a society where economic ruin was common, the fact that Maurin was financially distressed is no doubt significant; the statement that he had "no visible means of support" could apparently apply to his emotional as well as his financial state.

The function of photographic portraiture as a consoling personal memento was never more obvious than when the subject of the portrait was no longer living. "Secure the shadow ere the substance fade," the most common advertising phrase of the daguerreian era, is candid in its suggestion of death. Photographers in California were, if anything, even more direct:

> Where is taught that blest art which keeps the absent near.
> The beautiful unchanged, — from Time's rude theft
> Guards the fresh tint of childhood's polished brow.
> And when love yields its idol to the tomb. Doth snatch a copy.[35]

In a similar piece of advertising doggerel, Robert Vance was explicit:

> Think not these portraits, by the sunlight made,
> Shades though they are, will like a shadow fade;
> No! when the lips of flesh in dust shall lie,
> and death's gray film o'erspreads the beaming eye,
> Then VANCE's pictures, mocking at decay,
> Will still be fresh and vivid as to-day.[36]

Writer Susan Sontag has pointed out that "all photographs are *memento mori*. To take a photograph is to participate in another person's (or thing's) mortality, vulnerability, mutability. Precisely by slicing out this moment and freezing it, all photographs testify to time's relentless melt."[37] Nineteenth-century photographers and their patrons seem to have had an intuitive grasp of this truth. Postmortem portraiture was already a well-established part of a daguerreian's trade on the East Coast; many even advertised it as a specialty. In California, the high mortality rate combined with the great distance from loved ones to ensure a steady demand for death portraits. During the great cholera epidemic, the San Francisco firm of

*Unknown maker*
**Spanish Woman**
*Sixth plate ambrotype*
*Collection of the Oakland Museum of California,*
*gift of Dr. Stanley B. Burns*

Johnson and Selleck even "erected a small bldg. at Yerba Buena Cemetery for the purpose of taking daguerreian views of [the] last resting place of [the] deceased to send east to relatives."[38]

In cases in which the body could not be photographed, distant families could always commission daguerreotypes at graveside, a practice that seems peculiarly Californian.[39] In one such image from the Stanley Burns Collection, the tombstone is plainly legible: "Sacred to the memory of Solomon Hartshorn / late of Milford M.E. / He died Sept. 26, 1852 / Age 42 yrs" (pl. 32). Hartshorn's brothers had apparently made the long journey to California to commission a group portrait at graveside, the only possible remaining token of their loved one. The emotional significance of this unusual portrait for friends and family back home can only be imagined.

Upon opening another surviving image (pl. 127), one is confronted with nothing less than an elaborate death memorial. The image shows three men posed next to the grave of Phillip A. Potter, who, a brief death notice pinned to the inside case cover informs us, was formerly of New Bedford, dying of "Panama Fever" at the age of twenty-one. The well-kept grave with its elegant stone and white picket fence lies in barren terrain, while three men doff their hats in respect. The velvet plush opposite the image contains a collection of comforting verses for California widows, with such titles as "Alone," "To my Wife," and "Lost Ones Love us Yet." A great deal of effort and expense has clearly gone into the creation of this image; large-plate daguerreotypes were expensive, particularly when commissioned as outdoor views. The image was most likely intended to be sent home, perhaps to a young widow. Are the men brothers, or fellow miners intending to create a lasting memorial? Everything about this object speaks eloquently to its purpose as a precious final memorial to a young man, dead in a distant land, far away from friends and family (the fact that he died of Panama fever suggests that he likely was not even able to begin mining). It is not necessary for us to indulge in the maudlin sentimentality of the accompanying poetry to be moved by the poignant immediacy of this evocative memento.

Perhaps because of the implicit suggestion of immortality in photography, several patents were issued for setting daguerreotypes in tombstones. A writer for *Hutchings' California Magazine* approved of this practice, noting that such images of the deceased's living features would improve the melancholy aura of cemeteries:

If on every tombstone there could be seen the life-likeness of the sleeper, as with sparkling eye, and noble mien, he walked "a man among men;" or of some gentle lady, whose kindly and generous impulses could be read in every feature of the "face divine;" or of the angel-child, whose joyous laugh, and innocent smile speaks of the loss to its bereaved and loving parents — and of its passage from earth to heaven — how much more inviting would then be the last resting places of the departed, — could we thus seek the "living" among the "dead," and on every tombstone see the living representative of the sleeper.[40]

In a remarkable illustration of the consoling power of photography, California immigrants were even known to carry daguerreotypes to the grave. When city officials began removal of Yerba Buena Cemetery to make room for a public park in 1866, numerous bodies had to be relocated. The oldest cemetery in San Francisco, Yerba Buena was established "during the years 1850 and 1851, when the rush to California was greatest; when privation, destitution and death were common; and when, to increase the mortality, cholera visited the coast and wrought a terrible work of havoc among its inhabitants, [and] the 'community of the dead' increased at a fearful rate." A reporter for the *Alta California* was present when one of the coffins was opened:

> The clammy outlines of a female face, once beautiful, were for a moment visible, but remained so only a moment after the air had reached them. The remains of a pillow, stuffed with feathers, were under her head, and on her breast a daguerreotype in an unusually excellent state of preservation. We were permitted to carry off this valuable token, and have it now in possession to be seen by those who may wish to look upon it. It could be easily recognized by any one who had an acquaintance with the lady while she lived. . . . In gazing upon this surviving relic, our heart was touched.[41]

The heartrending significance attained by likenesses of deceased forty-niners is poignantly illustrated by a surviving image of a miner named William McKnight (pl. 31). At first glance a typical "forty-niner" portrait, slightly ludicrous in its earnest ferocity, the daguerreotype is accompanied by a series of letters that vividly convey the importance of the "best likeness." Like so many argonauts before him, McKnight had failed at mining, become disillusioned, and ultimately fallen ill. The association of a daguerreotype with personal mementos such as a lock of hair and the sense that the photograph was somehow an actual relic of an individual have never been more forcefully expressed. The first letter, from McKnight to his mother, is dated July 11, 1852:

> I write to you in great pain being unable to sit up for more than a few minutes at a time; this is the only letter I have written to St. Louis since I arrived here, I have always waited to get better but have grown worse every day. . . . You have heard of our great tribulations. We can only say the Lords will be done. I can't write about it. It oppresses me so to think what will become of my poor mother, wife & children. . . . I am here with a spanish woman at $12. per week living on borrowed money. If I don't improve in a short time I shall go to my wife.

Later, on July 18, he wrote: "I am this day thirty-five years old. I am now five hundred miles away from my wife and not a person about me who would do any thing without pay — The mail is about to close and I must bid Farewell *perhaps forever*. I can't say any more Farewell — God bless you is the prayer of your dying Son William."

*James May Ford (1827–c. 1877)*
**Portrait of a Boy Wearing Hat Standing Near Wheelbarrow, Pick, and Rifle**
*Half plate daguerreotype*
*Collection of the J. Paul Getty Museum*

Then a note from his wife, Margaret, explains McKnight's fate to his mother:

Alas he is gone. Died last night about ten oclock. You would scarcely have known him he was so changed. It will be some consolation to you to know that everything was done that could be. He had the best physicians but it was the Lords will to take him and we can only say the Lord hath given and the Lord hath taken away blessed be the name of the Lord. You will find a lock of his hair.

Then, remembering a daguerreotype of her husband, she gets to the crux of the letter:

I have always felt a strong desire to have the picture you sent to your sister. It is the only good one that has ever been taken and I would not have given it to any one but you. If you will write and ask for it for me I shall be very grateful indeed. You have the next best picture. I have none that is at all a likeness. You know your sister cant care much for it and I would give anything to posses it. Louise and George are well and send their love to you. William will be buried tomorrow. The mail closes tonight. Oh how terrible is it to see the grave close over those you love. I cant write more. I should be glad [to] have you write to me.

And finally, in postscript: "(Do try and get me that picture. Margaret)"[42]

By the late 1850s, the gold rush and the daguerreotype were both on the wane, victims of new technologies and economic forces. Now the thirty-first state, California was admitted to the Union as part of a compromise over the expansion of slavery and was happy to shake off its unruly frontier image. The nation at large had shifted its attention to the deepening sectional conflict that would soon combust into civil war. Yielding to market forces that favored the cheaper and less fragile paper prints, most California photographers made the change to the new collodion wet-plate process. Like many of his colleagues, San Francisco daguerreian William Shew noted the growing popularity of the new images, but found them inferior to daguerreotypes in beauty: "Paper and glass photographs have attracted more attention for the last year or two in the United States than previously; and it is probable that with greater improvements, of which they are capable, they will be more patronized. Yet they are not equal in appearance and beauty of finish to daguerreotypes, and probably will never become so, as the paper surface is not capable of receiving that polish which the silvered plate receives in daguerreotypes."[43]

In 1860 the *Sacramento Democrat*, in a report on the fine arts display at the state fair, could relate, "Mr. Shew has a show case, a frame of beautifully executed specimens of the daguerreotype, an art almost become obsolete."[44] That an invention described just a few years earlier as "one of the most beautiful discoveries of the age"[45] should so quickly and unceremoniously fade into obsolescence is not surprising considering the mood of the day. To most Americans, the new processes were yet another example of the technological "improvements" that the nation had routinely come to expect. Daguerreians like Shew could at least console them-

*Robert H. Vance (1825–1876)*
**Man, Woman, and Child** (**three generations?**)
*Quarter plate daguerreotype*
*Collection of Peter E. Palmquist*

selves that "on the whole, the progress of the photographic arts has been astonishing, and promises much for their future usefulness and prosperity. They are yet in their infancy, and no one can predict the beautiful improvements yet to be accomplished in them." [46]

He did not speak of what had already been accomplished. Ever forward-looking, like most Americans of 1850, Shew preferred to focus on the future. The remarkable photographic record of the gold rush produced by Shew and his fellow daguerreians was not systematically produced, collected, or deposited in government archives like the federally sponsored images of the Great Depression a century later. The visual history of the gold rush seen in these pages was left instead to be found among the private effects of thousands of gold seekers, ordinary men and women who had left home and family for the promise of instant wealth on a distant shore. The desperate eagerness with which the argonauts obtained these images is a tribute to the ultimate ability of cased images to comfort the displaced immigrant and to console loved ones left behind. Created for private purposes of sentiment and filial connection, California daguerreotypes have nevertheless survived to constitute a graphic and moving record of one of the great events of American history, surviving as mementos of silver and gold.

### NOTES

1   Robert Taft, *Photography and the American Scene: A Social History, 1839–1889* (New York: Macmillan, 1938; reprint, New York: Dover, 1964), 69; and Beaumont Newhall, *The Daguerreotype in America*, 3d rev. ed. (New York: Dover, 1976), 83.

2   Newhall, *The Daguerreotype in America*; Richard Rudisill, *Mirror Image: The Influence of the Daguerreotype on American Society* (Albuquerque: University of New Mexico Press, 1971); and John Wood, ed., *America and the Daguerreotype* (Iowa City: University of Iowa Press, 1991).

3   Wood, *America and the Daguerreotype*, 15.

4   Kevin Starr, *Americans and the California Dream, 1850–1915* (New York: Oxford University Press, 1973), 57.

5   Rudisill, *Mirror Image*, 233.

6   J. S. Holliday, *The World Rushed In: The California Gold Rush Experience* (New York: Simon and Schuster, 1981), 62.

7   George D. Dornin, *1849–1879 Thirty Years Ago: Gold Rush Memories of a Daguerreotype Artist*, ed. Peter E. Palmquist (Nevada City, Calif.: Carl Mautz Publishing, 1995), 4. After a try at mining, Dornin opened a daguerreotype studio in Grass Valley.

8   Unidentified New York newspaper, quoted in the *Green Bay (Wis.) Advocate*, February 22, 1849, which is in turn quoted in John Adams-Graf, "In Rags for Riches: A Daguerreian Survey of Forty-Niners' Clothing," *Dress* 22 (1995): 60.

9   William Welling, *Photography in America: The Formative Years, 1839–1900, A Documentary History* (New York: Crowell, 1978), 69.

10  Holliday, *The World Rushed In*, 80.

11  Fanny Boardman to William Boardman, n.d. (1851), Boardman Papers, Oakland Museum of California.

12 Wood, *America and the Daguerreotype*, 257.

13 T. A. Barry and B. A. Patten, *Men and Memories of San Francisco in the Spring of '50* (San Francisco: Bancroft, 1873), 143–44.

14 Holliday, *The World Rushed In*, 59.

15 Starr, *Americans and the California Dream*, 111.

16 Bayard Taylor, *El Dorado; or, Adventures in the Path of Empire* (1850; reprint, New York: Knopf, 1949), 47.

17 Holliday, *The World Rushed In*, 53.

18 *Humboldt Times*, November 18, 1854, quoted in Peter E. Palmquist with Lincoln Kilian, *The Photographers of the Humboldt Bay Region, 1850–1865* (Arcata, Calif.: Peter E. Palmquist, 1985), 78.

19 Barry and Patten, *Men and Memories*, 143, and William Shew, advertising broadside, "To the Babies of San Francisco," Bancroft Library, University of California, Berkeley.

20 *Shasta (California) Courier*, October 29, 1853.

21 Ibid.

22 Martha A. Sandweiss, Rick Stewart, and Ben W. Huseman, *Eyewitness to War: Prints and Daguerreotypes of the Mexican War, 1846–1848* (Fort Worth: Amon Carter Museum; Washington: Smithsonian Institution Press, 1989), 48; and donor files, Oakland Museum of California.

23 Holliday, *The World Rushed In*, 80.

24 Fanny Boardman to William Boardman, August 3, 1851, and n.d. (1851), Boardman Papers.

25 *Photographic and Fine Art Journal* 8, no. 1 (January 1855), quoted in Rudisill, *Mirror Image*, 217.

26 [William] Shew, "Photography," *The Pioneer or California Monthly Magazine* 2 (July 1854): 34.

27 *Trinity Journal*, May 22, 1858, quoted in Palmquist and Kilian, *The Photographers of the Humboldt Bay Region*, 94.

28 *San Francisco Alta California*, January 5, 1853.

29 *Humboldt Times*, April 14, 1860, quoted in Palmquist and Kilian, *The Photographers of the Humboldt Bay Region*, 78.

30 *Humphrey's Journal* 5, no. 19 (January 15, 1854): 297, quoted in Rudisill, *Mirror Image*, 216.

31 The best-known example of this theme in popular culture is the daguerreotypist Holgrave in Hawthorne's *The House of the Seven Gables*. There are numerous others; see, for example, Alan Trachtenberg, *Reading American Photographs: Images as History, Mathew Brady to Walker Evans* (New York: Hill and Wang, 1989), ch. 1, "Illustrious Americans."

32 Rudisill, *Mirror Image*, 42. Because Janin's comment was written before daguerreian exposure times were sufficiently fast to record the human face, the writer does not mention portraits.

33 *San Francisco Evening Bulletin*, May 9 and 12, 1856.

34 *San Francisco The Wide West*, May 20, 1856, reprinted in "An Arresting Case of Monomania in San Francisco," *The Daguerreian Annual* (1990): 51.

35 *Trinity Journal*, May 22, 1858, quoted in Palmquist and Kilian, *The Photographers of the Humboldt Bay Region*, 94.

36 *San Francisco Alta California*, January 5, 1853.

37 Susan Sontag, *On Photography* (New York: Farrar, Straus, and Giroux, 1977), 15.

38  *San Francisco Alta California*, September 23, 1855.

39  I know of five such graveside portraits, all of them taken in California.

40  "Daguerreotypes on Tombstones," *Hutchings' California Magazine* 1, no. 11 (May 1857): 519, quoted in Rudisill, *Mirror Image*, 218.

41  "Exhuming the Dead of Yerba Buena Cemetery — Interesting Particulars," *San Francisco Alta California*, February 15, 1866.

42  Richard S. Field and Robin Jaffee Frank, *American Daguerreotypes from the Matthew R. Isenburg Collection* (New Haven: Yale University Art Gallery, 1990), 56.

43  Shew, "Photography," 40.

44  *Sacramento Democrat*, September 1860, quoted in Wendy Cunkle Calmenson, "Likenesses Taken in the Most Approved Style: William Shew, Pioneer Daguerreotypist," *California Historical Quarterly* 56 (Spring 1977): 10.

45  Samuel F. B. Morse to *New York Observer*, quoted in Taft, *Photography and the American Scene*, 11.

46  Shew, "Photography," 40.

# Theatrical Narratives and the Documents of Dream

## California and the Great American Image

*John Wood*

*. . . der Gründung einer Paradiesstadt . . .*
Bertolt Brecht, *Aufstieg und Fall der Stadt Mahagonny*

The story of the California gold rush reads more like theater than history. It was as if the word went out — the word "gold" — and the world went mad. Multitudes of people, multitudes from the other side of the continent, from the other side of the planet even, simply put down their hoes, scythes, saws, razors, pens, nets, brushes, Bibles, the tackle of every trade, and headed for California. Husbands deserted their wives. The San Francisco harbor filled up with sleek, expensive ships deserted by their captains and crews. The American garrison at Monterey even deserted! People were so determined to get to California or bust that some actually resorted to cannibalism.[1] If they were fortunate enough to make it and find gold, they could then dine on watermelons at $16 each! Or they could indulge in prostitutes at $100 a night! San Francisco had its first Baptist church (pl. 134) go up nearly as quickly as its first whorehouse. French champagne and cognac flowed, though the streets were still unpaved. Funerals were interrupted for mourners to scratch through newly dug graves when the soil cast that special glint; miners dug up the floors of their own cabins; millionaires were made in a year, and paupers were often made more quickly than that. One miner wrote to his father in October 1849: "Fortunes are lost and won in five minutes. 36,000 dollars was risked upon the turn of a single card, and *lost*. . . . Money is *nothing* here; the tables groan under millions in gold and silver."[2]

The events of 1849 sound as if they were from a play by Bertolt Brecht. Sin, cash, heartbreak, pleasure — all the stuff of tumultuous times. San Francisco was Brecht's Mahagonny, a city also founded on a gold rush, the city of nets, of nightmare and daydream, of disillusion and delight. The woman who owns the hotel and bar called Here-You-May-Do-Anything declares, "The essence of gold is gin and whisky, girls and boys." In play after play — *The Rise and Fall of the City of Mahagonny, Happy End, The Seven Deadly Sins* — Brecht presented that same great human comedy that drove the gold rush. When we look into early photographs of California, we can see its very images and scenes played out, not on Brecht's stage but on the bright silver of the daguerreotype plate.

Look into the faces of William McKnight (pl. 31), George Baumford (pl. 3), the young miner with pan, pick, and shovel (pictured here), George Northrup with his money bag (pl. 58), or at portrait after portrait of men holding their pan and lump of gold. Why do these people look so unrelaxed, so unreal, so like characters caught up in drama, caught up in a play whose third act they have not yet read? It is not the daguerreotype's doing; that didn't stiffen them. There are countless daguerreotypes in which the subjects look as casual as

*Unknown maker*
**Miner with Pick, Pan, and Shovel**
*Sixth plate daguerreotype*
*Collection of Matthew R. Isenburg*

people in contemporary snapshots, but something is different here. These images are all theater. They might look factual, but they are illusions, created fictions, incomplete narratives; they are not really the sitters at all but the illusions that those long-gone individuals wanted to present.

We can look into them and easily see the roles they were playing. McKnight is dressed to look like a tough guy. His bright-red shirt, gun, and knife all say, "Watch out! I'm a killer." But poor William McKnight was one of the countless losers in the gold rush drama. Along with his daguerreotype came a letter to his mother. On July 11, 1852, he wrote to her from Los Angeles saying, "I have always waited to get better but have grown worse every day. . . . It oppresses me so to think what will become of my poor mother, wife & children." On July 18 he wrote: "I am this day thirty-five years old. I am now five hundred miles away from my wife and not a person about me who would do any thing without pay — The mail is about to close and I must bid Farewell *perhaps forever*. I can't say any more Farewell — God bless you is the prayer of your dying Son William." The letter was never sent by McKnight, but written on the same piece of paper is a letter from Margaret McKnight to her mother-in-law, dated August 13. It began, "Alas he is gone. Died last night about ten oclock."[3]

Confident George Baumford in his buckskins certainly looked the part of a Western hero in 1853 when his portrait was taken. An honest-to-goodness piece of Western theatricality like Buffalo Bill never looked better or more Western than Baumford. He had the look of a man who knew where he was going, but out on his ranch in 1853 he would never have guessed it would be Italy. From a note in the back of the daguerreotype case we learn that he was driven out by Indians in 1855 and eventually died in Florence.

As tough and resolute as the young man with his pan, pick, and shovel might look, he could just as easily be one of those many miners whom Luzena Wilson, a female forty-niner, described as they received letters from home: "Many a man whose daily life was one long battle faced with fortitude and courage, succumbed at the gentle touch of the home letters and wept like a woman. There was never a jeer at these sacred tears, for each man respected, nay, honored the feelings of his neighbor."[4] This boy's resolution may well have been for the camera alone.

And look at George W. Northrup. Do we really believe the bag is filled with gold, or is it just more theater, the narrative of his dreams? Were the big whisky jug, which seems so much like a prop, not beside him, we might be more tempted to believe the bag of gold isn't just another prop. It is interesting that the three principal things we see all lined up in a row in the daguerreotype — a jug of whisky, a man, and $90,000 — are those three essentials — *whisky, boy,* and *dollar* — that Jenny and her Here-You-May-Do-Anything girls in *Mahagonny* claim they must have or else they will die. And finally, in reality what we discover about this image is that it *is* pure theater; we are looking at a man who never made it to California. This image, owned by the Minnesota Historical Society, shows a Minnesota schoolteacher who decked himself out in the garb of a hard-drinking tough guy who found pay dirt but who never actually had the gumption to leave Minnesota, his slate board, his sums and differences.

*Unknown maker*
**Standing Miner with Blousy Shirt**
*Half plate daguerreotype*
*Collection of John McWilliams*

These images are all illusions. They admittedly are often beautiful photographic compositions, but they are not really about work or the life of the miner. Though they are all theatrical narratives, portraits of characters costumed for the roles they wanted to play, the narrative is always the same. It's not the American dream exactly, at least not the one about an open road traveled by tolerant, interracial comrades, the one Whitman dreamed of; it's the twenty-four karat American dream of quick and easy riches, a dream still omnipresent *now* the world over but one relatively recent in the world's history. Before the eighteenth century, the idea that wealth, like dreams, could be made on the breeze would have struck the Medici or any wealthy man as patently absurd, yet such a notion sparked and sustained the California gold rush. It even drove some miners to rhapsodize about gold and instant wealth with the fervor and language usually reserved for the deity:

> Upon Pacific's distant shores is heard a startling cry,
> A sound that wakes the nations up as swift the tidings fly;
> An El Dorado of untold wealth — a land whose soil is gold,
> Full many a glittering dream of wealth to mortal eyes unfold.
>
> O gold! how mighty is thy sway, how potent is thy rod!
> Decrepit age & tender youth acknowledge thee a God;
> At thy command the world is sway'd, as on the deep blue sea,
> The Storm King rules the elements that roll so restlessly.
>
> And see, the crowd is rushing now across the arid plain,
> All urged by different passions on, yet most by thirst of gain;
> And I, my home & native state, have left thy genial shade,
> To throw my banner to the breeze where wealth, like dreams, is made.[5]

Where did such ideas come from? Golden calves have, of course, been erected for a long time, but such notions of the easy acquisition of wealth were new. One cannot find anything like Robert Louis Stevenson's *Treasure Island* or Horatio Alger's rags-to-riches theme in literature before the eighteenth century. Chaucer's *Pardoner's Tale* does deal with three young men and a treasure beneath a tree, but it is really a typical medieval tale about an encounter with Death because the men soon kill one another for the gold. Later in the Renaissance, Sir Thomas More so disdains gold that the citizens of Utopia fashion their chamber pots from it and it is considered "the mark of infamy." But even by the eighteenth century one does not find instant, immediate, and easy wealth in the literature. Benjamin Franklin, in *Poor Richard's Almanack*, admonishes us to remember that time is money and that money is acquired only through hard work. Daniel Defoe's poor foundling Moll Flanders, in his novel of the same name, is often rich when she's a kept woman, a thief, and a good and virtuous wife, but she is just as often poor under all the same circumstances. Samuel Richardson's famous and im-

*Nathaniel Currier*
**The Way They Go to California, c. 1849**
*Hand-colored lithograph on paper*
*Collection of the Oakland Museum of California, Museum Founders Fund*
*Photo credit: M. Lee Fatherree*

mensely popular *Pamela* presents a poor serving girl who ends up rich, but only because she realized her virtue was a commodity and held out for the highest price. Tobias Smollett's comic portrait of a poor, bungling, none-too-smart but good-hearted Methodist preacher, *Humphry Clinker*, has Humphry find wealth at the end, but only because of the accidental discovery that he is the bastard child of a country squire.

Wealth had at least become a possibility, distant though it might have been, in eighteenth-century literature because wealth had become *makeable* in a way that it earlier had not been. In the previous century bourgeois capitalism had developed in Holland, and vast amounts of new money had been made by all those comfortable, corporate-looking groups of men that one sees in Rembrandt's work — the men at their table in *The Syndics*, the gentlemen watching the procedures in *The Anatomy Lesson of Dr. Tulp*, and so forth. And then, in 1720, millionaires, so to speak, actually *were* made overnight when the South Sea investments paid off. The growth of wealth is a democratizing process. Social barriers are broken down by the battering ram of cash. One critic said, "The eighteenth century was an age of the *nouveaux riches*, tinc-

*George Howard Johnson (c. 1823–?)*
**Miner with Scarf and Red Frock**
*Sixth plate daguerreotype*
*Collection of Stephen Anaya*

tured with the manners and tastes of those who have acquired wealth too easily and too rapidly." [6] Numerous contemporary writers uttered this same complaint. Lord Chesterfield described a typical nouveau riche to his son: "He is at a loss what to do with his hat, when it is not upon his head; his cane (if unfortunately he wears one) is at perpetual war with every cup of tea or coffee he drinks. . . . His sword is formidable only to his legs, which would possibly carry him fast enough out of the way of any sword but his own. His clothes fit him so ill, and constrain him so much, that he seems rather their prisoner than their proprietor." [7]

And later in the century Henry Mackenzie, the author of *The Man of Feeling* and certainly a man of good heart, complained of the same thing, but in even stronger language:

> The influx of foreign riches, and of foreign luxury, which this country has of late experienced, has almost leveled every distinction, but that of money, among us. The crest of noble or illustrious ancestry has sunk before the sudden accumulation of wealth in vulgar hands; but that were little, had not the dignity of deportment, had not the pride of virtue, which used to characterise some of our high-born names, given way to that tide of fortune, which has lifted the low, the illiterate, and the unfeeling, into stations of which they were unworthy. [8]

What Chesterfield, Mackenzie, and others found objectionable was the growth of the force that we delight in calling democracy but that, of course, has absolutely nothing to do with democracy. Something new was certainly afoot, and the United States eventually became its symbol and champion, but it wasn't democracy; it was just a new oligarchy, one based this time on wealth alone. The old one had been based on one's name, one's land, and finally one's wealth. Name became worthless and land relatively insignificant; wealth was now the only thing that counted. It was and still is a worldwide, ongoing process, especially now because of television, the World Wide Web, and the general growth of information. It has recently even subverted the two major social revolutions of the twentieth century. The collapse of Soviet and Chinese Marxism can curiously enough best be explained through Marxist analysis:

> What men are willing and able to put up with depends on what they are able to look forward to. . . . the urge to rise in the social scale arises only after the boundaries between the classes have begun to wobble . . . alienation from work . . . becomes . . . oppressive . . . [when] improvement of . . . [the worker's] position [is] within the realm of possibility. . . . In earlier historical periods he was objectively and materially no better off, but he was less aware of the wretchedness of his lot. [9]

Since the eighteenth century everyone has been increasingly aware of everyone else's lot and of the exact size of everyone else's lot. The desire for the same goods that others have and the knowledge of exactly what they have, coupled with those Romantic assumptions of fairness that we have all come to accept unquestioningly — equal pay for equal work, for example —

*Unknown maker*
**"Uncle Bill and Others at Mining"**
*Half plate daguerreotype*
*Collection of the Oakland Museum of California,*
*the S. H. Cowell Foundation*

set into motion the very forces that produced the Russian and Chinese revolutions and then finally uprooted them.

Those forces were at work early in the United States. And then in 1848 there came an amazing historical accident at a sawmill on the American River. Now anyone, even someone with no corporation in Amsterdam, with no South Sea stocks, with nothing but the determination to go to California, could be rich. A person didn't even have to have the money to get there! Companies offered to give free passage in return for a percentage of the individual's earnings over the next two years. And one didn't even have to go into gold mining to find gold. Elisha Crosby, a lawyer, noted that three potatoes, two small onions, and two small carrots cost $5, and so "Judge White of San Jose put in a little garden patch of onions that year [1849] and said that his crop netted him over $12000." [10] Luzena Wilson and her husband, whose name she never even mentioned in her memoir of the gold rush, arrived in Sacramento on the last day of September 1849. "The night before I had cooked my supper on the campfire, as usual," she wrote, "when a hungry miner, attracted by the unusual sight of a woman, said to me, 'I'll give you five dollars, ma'am, for them biscuit.' It sounded like a fortune to me, and I looked at him to see if he meant it. And as I hesitated at such, to me, a very remarkable proposition, he repeated his offer to purchase, and said he would give ten dollars for bread made by a woman, and laid the shining gold piece in my hand." With a $700 loan that she took out in Sacramento, she bought the El Dorado Hotel in Nevada City. In six weeks she paid back the loan and soon had from seventy-five to two hundred boarders a week at $25 per week each. Wilson began her memoir by saying: "The gold excitement spread like wildfire, even out to our log cabin in the prairie, and as we had almost nothing to lose, and we might gain a fortune, we early caught the fever."[11] Her logic is the same logic that has spoken to millions since 1849, and her fever is the fever of the modern world.

The California gold rush was not an isolated American event. The world was small enough in 1849 for the word to speed quickly round the globe, and it altered the world because it altered expectations of wealth as no previous event ever had. And it did make America seem like a promised land. The gold rush excited and thrilled the entire world — except for one man, the one man who most profoundly understood its consequences: Karl Marx. Marx was deeply depressed by the events in California and realized that they would undermine the revolution. The people whose faces look out at us from those California daguerreotypes were never going to be revolutionaries.

What they were going to be was the stuff of myth. In "American Destiny or Manifest Mythology," I wrote:

Nowhere was a mythology more manifest than on the frontier because nowhere was a mythology more needed. Our myths are the great structures we try to hang our own smaller lives upon in order to give meaning to them or make them bearable. In our myths we are heroic and larger than life; in our personal journals we weep with homesickness, worry about loss, . . . and are as human as everyone else. However, we do rise to our myths, and in doing so we find ourselves cloaked in our destiny. . . . [In these daguerreotypes we see] . . . the self-image, that is within an individual's potential. The mythology was manifest on their very faces, and that mythology shaped their destinies.[12]

They may look to us as if they were acting a part, and they may indeed have been acting a part, but they looked as if they believed in it, even if it did no more than give them the courage to continue the adventure they had set out upon.

The scenic images and group portraits present something of the same thing. It is clearly documentary photography; seldom is there any attempt to achieve an aesthetic or painterly image — even though there had been such a tradition in daguerreotypy from its inception and even though the daguerreotype process resulted in perhaps the most physically beautiful of all the camera's images. These early California scenes actually are often quite ugly — awful pits and scars on the landscape filled with men — and women — scratching away at the earth,

*Unknown maker*
**Log Cabin with Covered Wagon**
*Quarter plate daguerreotype*
*Collection of Matthew R. Isenburg*

the foreshadowing of frightening things to come, the price of the dream. The towns are usually no more than rows of shacks or some hastily thrown up storefronts offering meals and miners' tools. The life looks mean and hard, hard as in Mahagonny where the worst crime was "no dough" and the worst criminal was the man who couldn't pay his bills.

But as mean and hard as it might look, it looks nothing like the other great photographic documentation of gold fever — Sebastião Salgado's horrific picture of the mines and miners of Serra Pelada in northern Brazil.[13] What has changed in less than a century and a half? The pits are deeper and the numbers working in them far more vast. The pits are in fact so deep and the numbers so vast that the humanity is lost in the sweep of the image. We could be looking at bugs, or in some cases simply distant dull-gray stones. But that is not the real difference between Salgado and the daguerreotypists of the California goldfields.

*Sebastião Salgado*
**Serra Pelada Gold Mine, Brazil, 1986**

There is a hopelessness evident in all the Serra Pelada pictures; it's even more poignant and desperate in the close-ups. We know that even if a particular miner's bag of clay has a few grains or maybe an ounce of gold in it, his life will be no different. He works without hope. No vein will be his to mine. He will never be able to bring his family there. He will never be rich, never have even a good house, much less a mansion, never be free from worry. All possibility evaporated when he arrived. *Lasciate ogni speranza voi ch'entrate!* Serra Pelada is hell, as hellish as anything Dante dreamed, but what else lay before the Brazilian miner as possibility? Two out of every three Brazilians are malnourished. Brazil is a country of sixteen million abandoned children. And on and on go the statistics of hopelessness. When we look at Salgado's photographs of Serra Pelada, we know that everyone we see will live miserably until he dies miserably.

But that is not what one sees in the faces of the California argonauts. In fact, that very word, "argonaut," a word they chose for themselves and a word that characterizes their self-image as men and women of myth and destiny who drove their Argos out toward the gold fleeces of their dreams, epitomizes the difference in then and now. Then there was hope and those mythic structures for them to hang their lives upon; now the very smile of antiquity mocks us:

> He stands and smiles a smile to stun our sight.
> His Attic lips reveal antiquity's disdain
> For . . . the blight
> Of brutish air, a blighted future's trashed terrain. . . .
>
> Could Kroisos stand and rise to song, his lips would still remain
> Fixed in perpetual disdain.[14]

Could anyone today really believe that there is anything in the world that could possibly happen to improve the lot of the Serra Pelada miners or the children of the poorest of the Third World or the impoverished thug-teens of the Third World ghettos of American cities? Individually we have hope, and individually the lucky ones of us can structure our lives around the myths that will give them meaning, but without hope no one can afford the luxury of myth. Without hope the only thing that drives the individual is instinct, the instinct to survive, an instinct that will accept debasement so long as there is breath. But once, the hope and the potential were there for everyone — or nearly everyone. Blacks and Indians, of course, were excluded, except in the rarest of cases. But now the categories of exclusion transcend race. Unless one is born rich or into the comfortable middle class, there is little chance for real hope. There are no longer El Dorados or golden fleeces for the lowliest of these to aspire to, and though Harlem is hardly as horrific as Serra Pelada or the back streets of any place in Brazil, we cannot be content. The faces in those old daguerreotypes drive us to question ourselves, drive us not only to ask moral questions — which we must deal with in the solitude of our own hearts — but also to ask historical questions.

The gold rush was an exciting, grand, and wonderful moment in American history. When since have we been so thrilled? And why? What sort of frisson has gone out of our lives? The most important questions about gold rush photography to an American are, "How did such a spirit evaporate?" and "Can it be reinvigorated?" We can look at photographs all day long and talk about who made them and where they were made and how much they are worth, but all our discussion is meaningless unless we ask and answer the most existential questions posed by old photographs: "What happened? Where did it all go? Can we bring back anything now lost that was worth saving?" Photohistory that excludes such concerns is merely academic and self-indulgent. Why look into the past except to better understand the present and to improve it?

And so, how did that arrogant, argonaut spirit, that look of possibility that one sees in the gold rush images, evaporate? Can it be reinvigorated? The question of the manner of its reinvigoration is open to one's political persuasion. No American political party would claim that our grand and adventurous pre–Civil War spirit could not be reclaimed; all the parties

*Unknown maker*
**Miner with Shovel**
*Quarter plate daguerreotype*
*Collection of the Oakland Museum of California, museum purchase*

would merely argue over how it might be done. In truth it's about as reclaimable as the children of Brazil are savable. But no one who admits defeat can ever get elected. Everything must be possible, even when we know it isn't. That, however, is not so terrible a conundrum if continual striving is the result. The dilemma, however, usually results in cynicism; we think the incredible no longer possible and no longer believe that the act of striving is in itself a positive activity. It becomes only a waste of effort. To Jason and hundreds of generations of striving argonauts, everything once really did seem possible, but the possibility has now burnt off like morning fog in the sun's glare. Regardless of all the politicians' assurances, we can't re-create the past. But we can attempt to ascertain why certain changes took place, study them as cautionary tales for the future, and constantly strive both as individuals and as a society to do the impossible, whether we can achieve it or not.

People looked hopeful during the gold rush for the very reason Marx was depressed. The gold rush made it possible for people to change their lot in life without changing the fabric of society. This is made clear in image after image from the goldfields, all of which are so radically unlike Salgado's mining images that they hardly seem to be describing the same enterprise. Look at a large selection of the images. They are, of course, on their most mythic level, the chronicles of dreams, the transfixing of desires — those for wealth and success: enough money to go back home to Massachusetts and live a fuller life than before; or to bring the wife and children to California; or, though possibly mundane by comparison, to buy a night in a woman's arms or a dinner like you had not eaten since leaving your mother's kitchen or anything else that might help dispel the loneliness. But on a more prosaic level — on the most obvious visual level — they record a chronology of cooperation. Look at them: they are small groups of men working together — sometimes as few as four or as many as forty-two.

They represent a kind of early corporate mentality. These are pictures of mining companies, often with their homemade signs proclaiming their names (pl. 9). In some of the larger groups we are obviously also looking at hired hands, but in the smaller ones we know these people all have a stake in it together and are working for the good of the group. In a situation in which everyone owns a bit of the company, what's best for the company is best for the individual because what profits the company actually does also gain profits for the individual. Because they were working for themselves, these miners could find themselves in their labor, as grueling as it was, and not grow alienated from it.

These daguerreotypes, then, are little utilitarian vignettes, pictures of communes of possibility. And therein was the beginning of what I called the twenty-four-karat American dream. These people have the look of possibility in their eyes because things *were* possible for them, unlike the Brazilian miners. These nineteenth-century Americans had formed companies, business communes, that allowed the possibility for all of them to if not get rich at least become much better off by working for the good of the group. The fifty thousand Brazilians working the Serra Pelada pits have no similar stake in the mine; success for one is not success for all. Neither do they have a stake in anyone else's life. Nothing communal — except a

*Unknown maker*
**Gold Miners**
*Quarter plate daguerreotype*
*Collection of the Amon Carter Museum*

common dislike for the armed guards — is present there, where it is most needed. Necessity and utility brought the California miners together; they needed each other and could not succeed without each other. The paradigm on which the story of these California miners is based still exists today, but only as a cheap grotesque of what it once was. A company that sells stock and in which many individuals own a share is something like some of these mining companies originally were. But today what might be best for Multinational Paper, Inc., which might be harvesting all the forests of the world, is certainly not best for the individual who holds only fifty shares. In fact, it's not even best for the individual who holds controlling shares, if he has children.

It is difficult now to find such expressions of hope as one sees on the many faces from varied social classes that appear in the California daguerreotypes. Group portraits today showing the same class composition would hardly reveal such hope. The possibility suggested in the gold rush images seems to most people impossible now. And why? Look at the pictures; compare California to Serra Pelada. It's obvious. It's the size. Most California gold mining

*Attributed to Joseph Blaney Starkweather (c. 1822 – ?)*
**Auburn Ravine in 1852**
*Quarter plate daguerreotype*
*Collection of the California State Library*

images show six to ten people working together, but in the Brazilian images thousands are shown descending into the pits. The world has grown too large; there are too many people; the planet cannot sustain the life. There are more have-nots than ever before. The sense of possibility suggested by the gold rush finally just evaporated because there was only so much gold, so much lumber, so much oil, so much whatever. What's left of it is now controlled by a few with millions employed under them who have no greater stake in going to work than the next paycheck. If that is all that compels one to work, then neither the work nor the life can be fulfilling. Dreams collapse in the collapse of possibility; hope evaporates and despair sets in.

Once small groups of men could fill an *Argo* and sail out. They might have been driven only by a dream of wealth, but it was still, by necessity, a dream of comradeship, and as such

*Unknown maker*
**Group of Miners**
*Whole plate daguerreotype*
*Collection of the California Historical Society*

it was the larger dream, the grander dream, the dream that Walt Whitman would dream of a society in which Chinese and Indians and blacks and whites could work together for a common good. We can see it in these images, and there is something ennobling and grand about them. They really are pieces of the Great American Image. Landscapes may have been wrecked and scarred. The westward movement nearly exterminated the land's Native people. San Francisco, like Mahagonny, was the Paradise city, that *"Paradiesstadt"* — but only on the surface, only from a distance. We know these things and can look back and condemn history's crimes and errors with all the arrogance of hindsight. But that should not obscure the grander thing that can also be seen here, a spirit of comradeship that made itself manifest in communal business ventures, ventures that joined the spirit of bourgeois capitalism to social reform. The common man and woman, the most ordinary individual, a person without even the money to get to California, the lowly peasant of centuries of European society, now for the first time in history could, through his or her own labor and the joining in compact with others, rise into a higher social class. It was the joint realization of a dream both of capital and of reform. And it would not be realistic to expect so golden a moment again.

But can't we recast something like that Great American Image on our faces today? Small economic communes certainly work now. There are food co-ops and similar enterprises across these states, but no one gets rich. The original spirit of the dream was gobbled up by bigness, and little people probably can't make it big today unless they are mining the field of technology. The goldfields have shifted, and actual gold is less golden than it once was. Technology, computers, information — these are the new mines. And wealth is certainly possible — though hardly for the Third World peasant. But the potential of wealth is possibly not the most important thing that one sees in the gold rush daguerreotypes.

It is hard to consider the gold rush or San Francisco of 1849 without thinking of the similarities to Bertolt Brecht's decadent city of Mahagonny, but Brecht's play ends in an apocalyptic chorus of everyone crying, "We can't help ourselves or you or anyone." We see nothing like that in the early daguerreotypes of the goldfields. In fact, what we see is the exact opposite. Those gold rush scenes show the clear image of cooperation in plate after plate. There one can often find blacks, women, Mexicans, Indians, Chinese, Frenchmen, and white American males all working side by side together (pl. 76). That was finally the real spirit of the gold rush and that is finally what the Great American Image truly is. It was once our image, and it would be to the good of us all to make it ours again — especially since we have the good fortune now to make it wider, more vast, and more embracing than ever.

## NOTES

1   See LeRoy R. Hafen and Ann W. Hafen, eds., *Journals of Forty-Niners: Salt Lake to Los Angeles with Diaries and Contemporary Records of Sheldon Young, James S. Brown, Jacob Y. Stover, Charles C. Rich, Addison Pratt, Howard Egan, Henry W. Bigler, and Others* (Glendale, Calif.: Arthur H. Clark, 1954), 291, where Jacob Stover records hearing two members of the Death Valley Company, which he had parted with previously, tell of their ordeal. He quotes them as saying, "The boys said we would have to draw cuts in the morning who should be killed to eat. As we did not want to be killed to be eaten or eat anybody, when we thought they were asleep we got up and traveled till day." They arrived at a lake and found Indians "there catching fish and drying them. They saw our condition and put a guard over us. We would have killed ourselves drinking water and eating fish, which they had lots of dried. They kept us three days and then put us on a horse apiece and sent an Indian to guide us into California. That is how we got in." Even though we might recall the tragedy of the Donner Party of 1846, the idea of cannibalism is so horrendous and difficult to comprehend that I thought that, even in the midst of a general introductory paragraph, a footnote was warranted here. Sources for the other factual details may be found in John Wood, "American Destiny or Manifest Mythology: Some Historical Considerations of the Western Image," in John Wood, ed., *The Photographic Arts* (Iowa City: University of Iowa Press, 1997).

2   Alfred Doten, *The Journals of Alfred Doten, 1849–1903*, ed. Walter Van Tilburg Clark (Reno: University of Nevada Press, 1973), 1:52–53.

3   Richard S. Field and Robin Jaffee Frank, *American Daguerreotypes from the Matthew R. Isenburg Collection* (New Haven: Yale University Art Gallery, 1989), 56.

4   Luzena Stanley Wilson, *Luzena Stanley Wilson '49er: Memories Recalled* (Mills College, Calif.: Eucalyptus Press, 1937), 17.

5   Quoted in Vincent Geiger and Wakeman Bryarly, *Trail to California: The Overland Journal of Vincent Geiger and Wakeman Bryarly*, ed. David Morris Potter (New Haven: Yale University Press, 1945), 94–96.

6   Jay Barrett Botsford, *English Society in the Eighteenth Century* (New York: Macmillan, 1924), 254.

7   *Letters to His Son* (London: Dent, 1963), September 27, 1749, 123.

8   *The Lounger*, no. 100 (December 30, 1786), in *The Works of Henry Mackenzie Esq.* (Edinburgh: James Ballantyne, 1808), 28.

9   Arnold Hauser, *Mannerism* (New York: Knopf, 1965), 1:100.

10   Elisha Oscar Crosby, *Memoirs: Reminiscences of California and Guatemala from 1849 to 1864*, ed. Charles Albro Barker (San Marino, Calif.: Huntington Library, 1945), 111–112.

11   Wilson, *Luzena Stanley Wilson '49er*, 9, 28, and 1.

12   "American Destiny or Manifest Mythology," 16.

13   See Eduardo Galeano and Fred Ritchin, *An Uncertain Grace: Photographs by Sebastião Salgado* (New York: Aperture, 1990).

14   John Wood, "Elegiac Ode," from *In Primary Light* (Iowa City: University of Iowa Press, 1994), 58.

# The Sad but True Story of a Daguerreian Holy Grail

*Peter E. Palmquist*

FOUND!

ROBERT H. VANCE'S DAGUERREIAN PANORAMA OF
THE CALIFORNIA GOLD FIELDS!

This headline speaks of an event that never actually happened, but it could have. The safe recovery of Vance's *Views in California*, a three-hundred-plate daguerreotype "panorama" of San Francisco and "the diggin's," would be an unimaginable asset in showing sites and events that have intrigued researchers of gold rush–era California for almost 150 years. It could also be worth tens, if not hundreds, of millions of dollars today.

This essay is an overview of one of photography's most significant mysteries: what we know and what we don't know about this extraordinary photographer and his series of three hundred whole plate daguerreotypes made in 1850–51, which disappeared from sight about the time of the American Civil War. It is an account based on facts but spiced with dollops of speculation. In short, it is the stuff of legends replete with many unanswered questions. Who was Robert Vance and what caused him to travel halfway around the world to photograph a new frontier? How did he learn to make large-format daguerreotypes outdoors, apparently working alone and without access to a studio? Why did he elect to exhibit his daguerreotypes in New York, and how were they received?

Robert H. Vance was born in Maine in 1825.[1] As a young man he worked as a portrait photographer in Boston and New Hampshire during the mid-1840s. By February 1847 he had established himself as a daguerreian artist in Valparaiso, Chile.[2] He worked in South America until at least August 1850 before traveling to San Francisco by way of Panama City and Acapulco, Mexico. As a photographer in San Francisco, Vance subsequently founded a number of branch galleries in California, Nevada, and Hong Kong. By the mid-1850s his First Premium Gallery of San Francisco was considered the preeminent photographic establishment in the American West.[3] In many ways he was the Mathew Brady of the West. Because of overspeculation in mining stocks, however, Vance was forced to give up his San Francisco gallery about 1860, and afterward he lived in obscurity until his death on America's hundredth birthday, July 4, 1876.[4]

Our core story may have had its roots in Maine when Vance was still a youngster. Local newspapers sometimes featured accounts of such faraway and exotic places as Palestine, Hawaii, Haiti, and South America. In October 1839, for example, the local *Kennebec Journal* offered a detailed plan for developing a "Panama Canal" fully ten years before the California gold strike would send hordes of adventurers stumbling across the Isthmus of Panama.

*Unknown maker*
**Robert H. Vance, c. 1861**
*Albumen print carte-de-visite*
*Collection of the Oakland Museum of California,*
*gift of Mrs. Carolyn K. Louderback*

Likewise, by October 1841, the *Maine Democrat* had related the adventures of John Mix Stanley, who had taken his camera to Fort Gibson, Arkansas Territory, and photographed the local Indians. Later, when Vance moved to Boston, he gained access to an abundance of painted panoramas, a popular form of entertainment and forerunner of the newsreel or feature motion picture.[5] These panoramas were generally arranged as travelogues painted on giant canvas rolls, each scene transported from one side of the stage to the other by advancing the canvas on vertical rollers. The scenes were frequently accompanied by music and/or explanatory narrative. It is highly probable that Robert Vance attended one or more such showings, perhaps making mental notes on the effectiveness of the technique for explaining faraway events to a large audience.

Like many of his contemporaries, Vance made most of his income from daguerreian portraiture. During the 1840s, outdoor work was generally limited to assignments within easy reach of a photographer's studio and usually pictured a new storefront, home, or other human-centered improvement. Pure landscape photography was rare indeed. As far as is known, Vance never offered outdoor daguerreotypes before his arrival in South America. In August 1848, however, he journeyed to the silver mining region of Copiapo, capital of Atacama Province, known as the "Queen of Chilean Mining." Vance set out on his tour alone, taking one of the intercoastal steamers. After two days at sea, he arrived at the tiny port of Caldera, and from there he traveled the remaining fifty miles to Copiapo in a stagecoach. He probably remained in Copiapo for several weeks. Presumably his clients ranged from wealthy mine owners to the miners themselves.[6] While we have no direct evidence, it is logical that Vance did at least some outdoor photography. If so, the uncanny similarities between the mining sites of Copiapo and those of California cannot be ignored.

Although Vance was far removed from Boston, he was not isolated from world events. Intercoastal steamers brought regular supplies of newspapers and journals, many only a few weeks old. The discovery of gold in California on January 24, 1848, was international news and quickly flooded every ship plying the Cape Horn route with men who had dropped everything in order to see the "Elephant" (a euphemism for gold) firsthand. Thus, the coastal ports of South America were an ideal place from which to watch the unfolding drama of the new El Dorado. Meanwhile, travel panoramas continued to be produced. In March 1848, *Bayne's Gigantic Panoramic Painting of a Voyage to Europe* was showing at Amory Hall in Boston.[7] October saw the arrival of *Donnavan's Great Serial Panorama of Mexico!!!* This modest show occupied 21,000 feet of canvas.[8] Such exhibitions fueled the imagination of viewers and created a longing to see "the thing itself." Moreover, people were willing to pay good money for these public titillations, a fact that would not have been lost on the enterprising Robert Vance.

The California gold strike had an immediate impact on panorama production. In September 1849 a *Voyage Around Cape Horn* was already being exhibited in New York. The following spring the Emmert and Penfield *Panorama of the Gold Mines of California* was unrolled at Gothic Hall, Brooklyn.[9] James Wilkins's *Moving Mirror of the Overland Trail*, painted in Peoria

*Frederick Coombs (1803–1874)*
**Looking South on Montgomery Street, San Francisco, 1850**
*Half plate daguerreotype*
*Collection of the George Eastman House*
*San Francisco as it looked at the time of Vance's arrival.*

by a St. Louis artist, began its tour in September 1850. Beale and Craven's *Voyage to California and Return* appeared at Stoppani Hall, New York, in November 1850.[10] While it can't be proved, it is likely that Vance would have learned of these highly publicized panoramas or at least would have heard rumors that such activity was under way.

Aside from their shared focus on the California gold rush, the panoramas mentioned above had one thing in common — they were composed of sketched or painted images. Not only was a painting subject to interpretation by the artist, but it was probable that many of the scenes were fanciful, perhaps even invented by artists who had never been west of New York. Vance would later refer to these productions disparagingly as "exaggerated and high-colored sketches, got up to produce effect."[11]

The exact moment when Vance decided to undertake a panorama of daguerreotype images is not known, but it was not later than mid-1850. He obviously felt that a daguerreotype would have the accuracy and authenticity that were lacking in painted illustrations. His views, as he would later indicate in the preface to his exhibition catalog, were, "as every daguerreotype must be, the stereotyped impression of the real thing itself."[12]

There were comparatively few precedents for daguerreotype panoramas — consisting of multiple plates designed to be viewed together — before 1851. The most obvious example, which still survives today, is a series of eight daguerreotypes of the Cincinnati waterfront by Charles Fontayne and William Porter taken on September 24, 1848. The plates were mounted end to end in a single frame more than eight feet long.[13] While it is unclear whether Vance was personally aware of the Cincinnati series, he did employ similar techniques. He also planned to follow the "travelogue" format. The best example, and one that Vance would emulate, was Emmert's *The Gold Mines of California*, which was so arranged that the audience could view each of the principal features along the most common route to the California goldfields, from the Isthmus of Panama to Acapulco to the "Entrance to the Bay of San Francisco," and on to the goldfields themselves.[14] Unlike his "painted panorama" competitors, however, Vance appears to have undertaken his panorama in secrecy, a wise decision in light of the number of new productions under way by early 1851. The most threatening, from Vance's point of view, was John Wesley Jones's *Pantoscope of California*, which was to be based on a series of daguerreotypes starting in California and extending eastward along overland trails.[15]

When Vance set out for California, he was no longer the same young man who had left Boston in 1846. His life in South America had transformed him into a robust, westering adventurer. Also, his recent experiences with Hispanic customs, foods, folklore, language, and philosophy of life would have been especially helpful in a land formerly under Spanish control. Vance probably departed Valparaiso during the Chilean winter of 1850, possibly in August. The first leg of his journey lasted about nine days, with stops at a number of small ports before arriving at Callao, Peru.

Unlike most travelers to California, Vance proceeded fairly slowly, obviously working on his daguerreian panorama. He already had at least three images of Valparaiso (catalog nos. 109, 130, and 131) in his possession. The newest image would be taken in Peru, where he apparently traveled to the remote city of Cuzco, some 660 miles southeast of Lima. Capital of the vast Inca empire, Cuzco was a mile-high city, the center of which was dominated by the cathedral, a landmark that became view number 108 in his collection. Returning to Callao, he continued his journey to Panama, arriving during the rainy season (annual precipitation of seventy inches is customary). High humidity, coupled with an average temperature of 84 degrees, must have made his daguerreotype work very difficult. Yet, despite these inconveniences, he made at least three successful daguerreotype images, one of which was a multiplate panorama (nos. 105, 106, and 107). Approximately one week later he arrived in Aca-

*Unknown maker*
**San Francisco and the Bay**
*Four whole plate fragments of incomplete, noncontiguous panorama*
*Collection of the Society of California Pioneers*

pulco, Mexico. In his 1851 catalog, numbers 103 and 104 represent Acapulco overviews. Visible in the harbor were the steamers *Panama* and *Sea Bird*, one of which may have carried Vance northward to California.[16]

When Vance finally reached California, he was already carrying the first nine daguerreotypes of his *Views in California* panorama. Collectively, these images taken along the coast of South America and in Peru, Panama, and Mexico would have presented a vivid glimpse of one of the major pathways to California: the sea route by way of Cape Horn.

In California he would have to compete with a number of competent daguerreotypists already working in San Francisco and the goldfields. There seemed to be no mention of his arrival in San Francisco and certainly no discussion of his plans to produce a daguerreian panorama. In fact, it was not until January 21, 1851, that his presence was finally confirmed in an advertisement in a local newspaper: "NEW DAGUERREOTYPE ROOMS. R. H. VANCE invites public attention to the splendid Miniatures which he is now executing at his rooms on Clay Street, over Steadman & White, jewelers, and nearly opposite the Adelphi Theatre." The notice related his long tenure "in some of the principal cities of the United States and South America." His offerings included daguerreotype copies of "Paintings, Drawings, Plans or Machinery." It is the final line of his advertisement, however, that interests us most: "Views taken of the city, or any part of it, at the shortest notice."[17]

During 1850 nearly 36,000 persons arrived in San Francisco by sea. Whereas in 1848 there had been only about 600 inhabitants living in a few tents and rude buildings, there were now more than 25,000 residents in the city. San Francisco was in a constant flux of building and change, and Vance was ideally suited to document these changes with his large daguerreotype camera.[18] The exact date of his arrival in California is still unknown. He was not listed

in San Francisco's first city directory, published effective September 1, 1850.[19] An assumption that he began his California odyssey between September 1850 and January 1851 (the date of his first advertisement), would be consistent with a comment in the local *Alta California* newspaper, about "Mr. Vance, the daguerrean artist, who operated here with so much success during the winter and spring of '51."[20] Exactly how much success can only be conjectured, but we do know that nearly forty images of San Francisco, all taken before May 4, 1851, were included in his finished panorama.

Vance's pre–May 4, 1851, views of San Francisco could have been taken at any point during his stay. We know, however, that the views made from the top of the Union Hotel could not have been obtained before November 7, 1850, the date of its opening. Vance was certainly in San Francisco on March 15, 1851, for he placed a new advertisement in the *Alta California*,[21] and it ran until the disastrous May fire. Thus, he may well have been the mysterious figure mentioned in the *Alta* of March 10: "Yesterday morning, during the meeting on the plaza [Portsmouth Square] a man was engaged upon the top of the California Exchange in taking a daguerreotype view of the crowd."[22]

Nearly eighty of the remaining titles of his *Views in California* were taken at inland sites, including the mines. Roughly seven geographical areas are represented (see appendix), which when taken together, form a loose circular loop beginning and ending in San Francisco. Most were accessible by inland steamer.[23] While it is possible that Vance made a single, all-encompassing trip to photograph these sites, it is equally likely that he made multiple trips. Benicia (nos. 93, 94, and 95) was on the way to Sacramento and other points, including Marysville and Stockton. Dateable events suggest that at least some of the daguerreotypes were taken during March and April 1851. Less certain, however, is how Vance was able to

The Second Great Fire which Followed in June

A LITHOGRAPHER'S STORY OF THE GREAT FIRE OF JUNE 22, 1851. The flames destroyed houses and merchandise valued at $3,000,000. It started on the west side of Telegraph Hill, near Broadway, and swept south along Stockton street, carried by a heavy gale. At that time the leading residence part of the city lay directly in its course, which explains the comparatively small loss. The fire companies of that day were manned by volunteers over a hundred men in each company, of business and workingmen, who pulled the engine by a long rope to the fires. In a conflagration like that in the picture the fire checking resources of the city were utterly inadequate, which explains the many big fires and immense losses during the pioneer period. The view is taken from Russian Hill. Many citizens watched the fire from this site, just as many residents did during the three days' burning of the city, April, 1906. The flag in the right center of the picture marks the site of the Plaza. In line with the flag is the famous El Dorado gambling house. To the right of the flag is the Union Hotel, a landmark in its day. This fire roused suspicion of incendiary origin. Business men started an inquiry, which later led to the formation of the Vigilance Committee of 1851.

residential sections suffered heavily. In their day those two fires were practically more destructive than the fire of April, 1906. But the pioneers of those days possessed all the grit and determination that distinguishes their descendants, and the hot ashes were scraped off the sites in order to hasten reconstruction on the properties. Loss $20,000,000.

There were big fires in 1855 and 1868, but their losses were incomparable with those of 1851, and residents took their losses stoically

*Unknown maker*
### Lithographer's Story of the Great Fire of 1851
*Photographic reproduction of lithograph*
*Collection of the Oakland Museum of California, gift of Herbert Hamlin*

obtain his views of the inland goldfields, given that large-format daguerreotypy in the middle of a gold frenzy would have been very difficult and that apparently (as far as we know) he worked alone.[24]

There were very good reasons for Vance's continued secrecy and for a hasty completion of his daguerreian panorama. In January 1851, for instance, a five-plate daguerreotype panorama of San Francisco was placed on public display. The images were half plate size and the maker was Sterling C. McIntyre. The *Alta California* was very enthusiastic: "Decidedly the finest thing in the fine arts produced in this city . . . this picture, for such it may be termed, although a first attempt, is nearly perfect."[25] The *Alta* further noted that the image was to be displayed at the upcoming "World's Industrial Convention," in London and speculated that "nothing there will create greater interest than this specimen of Art among us, exhibiting a perfect idea of the city which of all the world carries with its name abroad more of romance

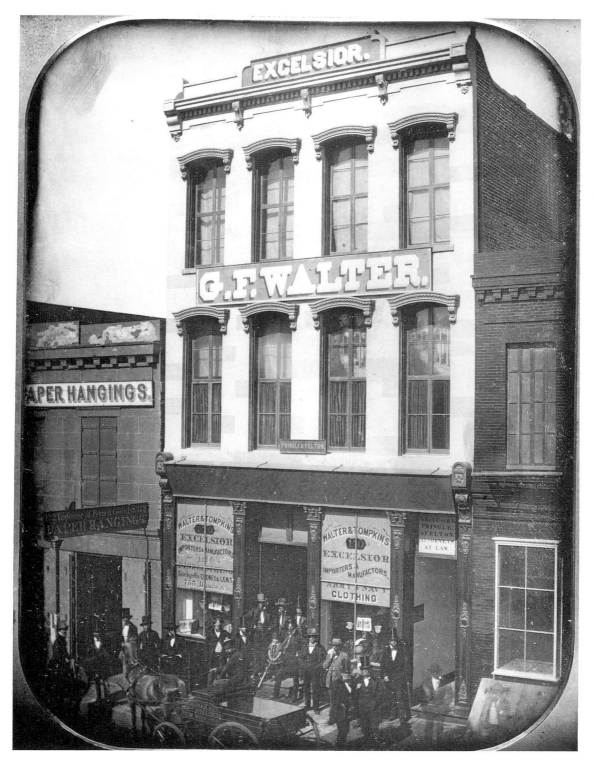

*Robert H. Vance (1825–1876)*
**Excelsior Building, Montgomery Street, San Francisco, 1856**
*Whole plate daguerreotype*
*Collection of Matthew R. Isenburg*
*This compelling image is one of the few surviving whole plate views by Vance.*

**Robert H. Vance and His Studio Staff, San Francisco, late 1850s**
*Albumen print carte-de-visite*
*Courtesy Peter E. Palmquist*

and wonder than any other. It is a picture, too, which cannot be disputed — it carries with it evidence which God himself gives through the unerring light of the world's great luminary." [26]

Meanwhile, yet another painted California panorama was under way. In Stockton, W. H. Cressy had begun *The Panorama of California,* and it was doubtless in progress at the very same time as Vance's visit to Stockton in the spring of 1851. Billed as the "Chef d'euvre" of panoramas — "Each view is 20 feet in length and 9 feet in height, and is executed in oil colors" [27] — Cressy's panorama was exhibited in California as early as June 1851. Likewise, details of John Wesley Jones's *Pantoscope* were announced as early as April, presumably to Vance's consternation: "Panorama of California and the Plains — We learn that a company of enterprising young artists are now engaged in taking daguerreotype views of San Francisco, San Jose, Stockton, and along the San Joaquin and Sacramento Rivers. About the 1st of June they start across the plains by the Great Salt Lake, taking connecting views through to Independence, Missouri. The Panorama will be painted from the daguerreotype views in Lowell, Mass., and will be the largest ever exhibited in the United States." [28]

Throughout the winter and spring of 1850–51, Vance was greatly aided by "the extreme salubrity of the [California] climate. . . . [The winter] was a remarkably dry and pleasant one, a striking contrast to the dreary winter of 1849–50." [29] It may be, however, that this mild winter was a contributing factor in the explosive San Francisco fire of May 4. It seems likely that Vance was away from the city at the time of the conflagration. If so, his timely absence may have saved much of his photographic equipment, which otherwise would have burned along with his gallery. Much of Clay Street was destroyed, especially the area where Vance's gallery was located. An account written at the time of the disaster described the holocaust:

> The sight was sad, afflictive, awful. Great masses of smoke ascended and rolled away, loaded with the wealth of men, the rewards of toil and danger, bearing far above the crumbling city great flocks and sheets of burning cinders. . . . Frame houses faded away like frost work. Brick structures became batteries of flame, and poured forth immense jets from their windows and doors. Iron and zinc curled up like scorched leaves, and sent forth their brilliant flames of green, blue and yellow tints, mingled with, and modifying the glare of the great red tongues of fire which flashed upwards from a thousand burning houses. [30]

View number 7 of Vance's panorama depicts a scene at the corner of Montgomery and Broadway Streets, four days after the May 4 fire. On May 9 he offered a $50 reward for information regarding the whereabouts of "TWO TRUNKS." One was described as "a light haired trunk, containing Daguerreotype cases, one whole plate tube [lens] marked Vaightland [*sic*] & Son, one pair of silver spurs, bridle and stirrups, taken from the Plaza in front of the Bella Union, early on Sunday [the day of the fire] morning." [31] Information concerning the trunks was to be delivered to the "Billiard Room in the Louisiana House." On May 18 Vance advertised: "Those who wish a Daguerreotype View of this city as it now is, can have it taken by leaving their order at the billiard room in the Louisiana House." [32] Vance was also present at the aftermath of the June 22, 1851, fire. In many ways, these twin tragedies formed a bizarre climax to his *Views in California*. Moving quickly, he transported his daguerreotypes to New York, likely by the fastest possible route, which was across the Isthmus of Panama.

By August Vance was in New York, where he spent $700 to have his daguerreotypes elegantly framed in rosewood. [33] Either shortly before or concurrently with the opening of his *Views in California*, he displayed a four-plate panorama of San Francisco at the exhibition of the American Institution. His fellow exhibitors included such well-known daguerreians as Jeremiah Gurney, Marcus and Samuel Root, Jesse H. Whitehurst, and George S. Cook. [34]

Vance's *Views in California* opened at 349 Broadway, "corner of Leonard Street and Broadway, over Mr. Whitehurst's gallery." [35] Jesse H. Whitehurst, a most enterprising daguerreian, had galleries in many East Coast locations, including Washington, Baltimore, Richmond,

# CATALOGUE

OF

# DAGUERREOTYPE PANORAMIC

# VIEWS IN CALIFORNIA.

By R. H. VANCE.

ON EXHIBITION AT

# No. 349 BROADWAY,

(OPPOSITE THE CARLETON HOUSE.)

NEW-YORK:
BAKER, GODWIN & COMPANY, PRINTERS,
TRIBUNE BUILDINGS.
1851.

*Robert H. Vance*
**Catalogue of Daguerreotype Panoramic Views in California 1851**
*Baker, Godwin and Company, Publishers, New York*
*Cover of exhibition catalog*

Norfolk, Petersburg, and Lynchburg, as well as New York City.[36] Vance's intentions were never better outlined than in the preface to his exhibition catalog:

> Within a few years attention has been particularly directed to California. The discovery of Gold, spread over an extent unparalleled in the history of the Precious Metals, has given it an importance in the eyes of the world, never before equalled in the annals of history. To such a pitch has public curiosity been excited, that the smallest item of news in regard to this newly discovered El Dorado, is eagerly seized upon. Much valuable information has been given in regard to the country, by several excellent works, but inasmuch as the sight of a place affords so much more pleasure, and gives so much better knowledge than the bare description possibly can, the Artist flatters himself that the accompanying Views will afford the information so much sought after. These Views are no exaggerated and high-colored sketches, got up to produce effect, but are as every daguerreotype must be, the stereotyped impression of the real thing itself.[37]

Early reviews from the photographic press were highly enthusiastic. The editor of the *Photographic Art-Journal*, for example, described the arrangement devised for the exhibition by the twenty-six-year-old daguerreian:

> There are over three hundred daguerreotypes so arranged that a circuit of several miles of scenery can be seen at a glance. They are the most artistic in design, and executed with skill, evincing, not only a perfect mastery of the manipulatory art, but an exquisite taste for the sublime and beautiful. On looking upon these pictures, one can almost imagine himself among the hills and mines of California. . . . Almost every variety of scenery is presented to the view. Three or four hours can be very profitably and amusingly spent in studying Mr. Vance's collection, and no Daguerreotypist, visiting the City of New York, should neglect the opportunity of seeing one of the most interesting exhibitions of Daguerreotypes ever presented to the inspection of the public of any country. Persons contemplating a trip to the gold regions should also avail themselves of Mr. Vance's instructions, as he is intimately acquainted with all the places of note in California, and takes pleasure in imparting any information desired by his visitors.[38]

The *Daguerreian Journal* commented on the great difficulty of Vance's undertaking, especially with regard to the accuracy and minute detail found in his pictures:

> We must say the operator has the proof of untiring industry and liberal enterprise in making such a display of Daguerreotypes. When we consider the disadvantage of operating in a tent or the open air, and in a new country, we are much surprised at such success; as a collection, we have never seen its equal, many of the pictures will compare with any taken with all the conveniences at hand. . . . Here we have every line faithfully portrayed and possessing a degree of minuteness in detail not to be equalled by the hand of man.[39]

*Alburtus Del Orient Browere (1814–1887)*
**View of Stockton, 1854**
*Oil on canvas*
*Collection of the Oakland Museum of California, Kahn Collection*
*Compare this painting to the descriptions in Vance's catalog numbers 11 and 12.*

The *Photographic Art-Journal* compared Vance's *Views in California* with the various painted panoramas currently available to the public. In the words of "one of our best landscape painters" (unfortunately not named): "Form, in color, is perhaps the greatest charm upon which the eye can dwell, therefore a panorama in distemper colors, should be considered of paramount importance to one produced by the Daguerreotype. We speak understandingly on this subject, and do not hesitate to say that Mr. Vance's views of California created in us a greater degree of admiration than did Banvard's or Ever's great productions of the Mississippi and noble Hudson." [40] The painter then turned to a lengthy discussion of the questions surrounding the relationship of detail and fidelity to nature, which had troubled painters ever since the earliest introduction of the daguerreotype process:

Detail . . . should be the principle aim of all artists, and if any desire to see this achieved to the highest state of perfection, let them call and examine the . . . productions of Mr. Vance. Not a blade of grass, nor the most minute pebble — hardly perceptible to the naked eye — nor the fibres of the bark of the tree — nor the myriads of tiny leaves that compose the clustering foliage — nor the silver stretches in the zig-zag ripple of the water as it glides gently on, or meanders among the rocks, washing up in its passage the little

1. *Wahla*, chief of the Yuba tribe,—civilized and employed by Mr. S. Brannan.   2. A partly civilized Indian.   3. A wild Indian.—From daguerreotypes by Mr. W. Shew.

**California Indians, from Lost Daguerreotypes by William Shew**
*Wood engraving*
*Courtesy Peter E. Palmquist*
*See numbers 57 and 69–72 in Vance's catalog.*

spangles of gold which have made California the great attraction of the whole world — but are wonderfully portrayed in these pictures in miniature most incomparable. . . . There is one [view] in particular, having in it a fallen tree over three hundred feet in length, sharp, angular rocks, etc., which we have no hesitation in saying, is the finest daguerreotype view ever taken.[41]

Truly, at least in the eyes of these critics, Vance had completely succeeded in capturing "the real thing itself." The paying public, on the other hand, was inexplicably uninterested. The New York newspapers were strangely silent about the exhibition, despite having previously devoted extensive coverage to both the May and the June San Francisco fires.[42] Vance's exhibit included firsthand evidence of the aftermath of these conflagrations, yet it seemingly passed without mention in the daily press.

*Unknown maker*
**Maidu Headmen with Treaty Commissioners**
*Half plate ambrotype*
*Collection of the George Eastman House*
*Compare Vance's catalog number 62 with this portrait of Maidu headmen.*

It was not that the Broadway site was a poor location for *Views in California*. Not only was this the center of both business and social activities, but on Sundays it was a popular promenade for New York's prominent citizens. Broadway was also the preferred location for daguerreian studios. In 1850 *Humphrey's Journal* remarked: "There is probably no city in the United States where the Daguerreian art is more highly appreciated . . . than New York." [43] So the question remains: what went wrong?

Speculation suggests that Vance may have simply arrived too late to partake of the excitement that had accompanied the news of the great San Francisco fires. It may be that he failed to hire a local promoter and, as a consequence, placed too much faith in the hope that recognition among his peers would translate into public interest. Or perhaps he simply charged too high an admission price. In any event, public response was vastly disappointing. Even the

*Photographic Art-Journal* felt obliged to comment: "Mr. Vance was disappointed in the realization of his hopes, and although they are among the best daguerreotype views ever taken, they failed to attract that attention necessary to the support of an exhibition of any character. Mr. Vance consequently closed his rooms in this city, and returned to California."[44]

Jeremiah Gurney, an important New York daguerreotype gallery operator, "added" Vance's collection of daguerreotypes to his gallery in 1852, and they are listed in his advertisements for that year.[45] That may have been a fortuitous move, since the 349 Broadway location was subsequently destroyed by fire and the *Views* might well have perished at that time.[46]

In February 1853 the *Photographic Art-Journal* advertised Vance's *Views in California* for sale, saying: "In procuring these views, Mr. Vance expended $3000, and the frames cost him $700 more. He is now desirous of selling them, and we are commissioned to dispose of them collectively, or in portions to suit purchasers."[47] The entire collection was offered for $1,500; half for $900; a quarter of it for $500; or one-eighth for $300.[48] Ultimately, the collection was offered at auction, "On the 20th of July, 7 1/2 p. m. at the auction rooms of Bangs, Brothers & Co., No. 18 Park Row, New York."[49] The successful bidder was daguerreian John H. Fitzgibbon of St. Louis, Missouri.[50]

Fitzgibbon apparently obtained the entire collection and immediately had it shipped to St. Louis. He now claimed that his gallery display of daguerreotype "specimens" exceeded one thousand images, collectively valued at more than $10,000.[51] By the spring of 1854 he advertised: "No Charge! to visit Fitzgibbon's immense collection of Pictures lit up at night with gas, and see those fine views of California and hundreds of other pictures too numerous to mention."[52] Vance's views were still on display at Fitzgibbon's studio in April 1856, when the *Photographic and Fine Art Journal* reviewed the establishment.[53] They have not been heard of since.

Dolores Kilgo, a scholar with a special interest in pioneer St. Louis photographers, has studied the relationship of Fitzgibbon to the "lost" Vance daguerreotypes:

> In the absence of later records linking the Vance collection to Fitzgibbon's establishment (either in the St. Louis press or in the photographic literature of the period), we can assume that the transfer of those plates to the St. Louis Museum was a permanent arrangement. Fitzgibbon apparently sold or loaned the views to J. P. Bates, the museum's "practical naturalist" and proprietor, sometime in the spring or summer of 1856. Unfortunately, little is known about this curious institution, which operated under changing management in various locations in the city until at least 1875.[54]

Over the years, many speculations have been set forth to account for the "Lost 300." The most credible suggest that they were destroyed by fire or through the vicissitudes of neglect and disinterest — perhaps donated to a scrap metal drive.[55] A happier thought is that the fabled *Views in California* still exist, lying merely forgotten in some St. Louis garret or basement hiding place, awaiting rediscovery.[56] Considering the superb level of excellence shown by Vance's surviving photography, the loss of his daguerreian panorama is without doubt one of

## GEN. JOHN A. SUTTER.

*[From an Ambrotype by R. H. Vance.]*

**Gen. John A. Sutter, from an Ambrotype by R. H. Vance**
*Wood engraving*
*Courtesy Peter E. Palmquist*
*Compare Vance's catalog number 129.*

*Robert H. Vance*
**James Marshall in Front of Sutter's Mill, Coloma, 1851**
*Albumen print copy (by Carleton E. Watkins) of lost daguerreotype*
*Courtesy Peter E. Palmquist*
*Could this print depict one of "the lost 300"?*

the greatest tragedies of photography. Even the most brief review of the titles listed in Vance's catalog — together with the statements of those who actually saw these images firsthand — confirms his *Views in California* as a historical treasure of untold value.

### CATALOGUE OF DAGUERREOTYPE PANORAMIC VIEWS IN CALIFORNIA 1851

The following listing from Vance's 1851 catalog sorts his titles into geographical clusters and presumed chronological order. The difference between the 131 views listed and the 300 claimed may be accounted for by the additional plates that made up each panorama and/or by multiple images listed under a single title. (View number 119 was apparently not assigned.[57]) Modern dating clues and subject notation have been added, in italics. Generally speaking, the South and Central American images probably date from the late summer or early fall of 1850 and the California views from the winter of 1850 through the end of June 1851.

I.  VALPARAISO, CHILE

*Technically speaking, the Valparaiso images could have been taken as early as the spring of 1847, the date of Vance's arrival in that city. It is likely, however, that they were taken not long before his departure for California, in the summer or fall of 1850 (see pl. 66).*

109  View of a portion of Valparaiso, S.A.

130  English Admiral's House, Valparaiso, S.A.

131  View of Valparaiso, from the American Consul's residence, showing Fort and Barracks in the distance.


II.  CUZCO, PERU

*Cuzco is some 660 miles southeast of Lima, Peru, and was the ancient capital of the Inca empire. The center of the town was dominated by the cathedral, which was begun by the Spanish architect Francisco Becerra around 1582. It is most likely that Vance would have undertaken this perilous journey from the seaport of Callao, a common landing place for intercoastal shipping.*

108  View of the Cathedral at Cuzco, Peru.


III.  PANAMA CITY, PANAMA

*The Cathedral of Panama was started in 1690 and completed in 1750. It features two large bell towers, and it was probably from this location that Vance was able to obtain his views of the city and several offshore islands.*

105  Panoramic View of Panama, taken from the Cathedral, showing the surrounding country, Island of Bogota, and others in the Pacific, ruins of various churches and monasteries.

106  View of the Cathedral.

107  View of the Islands opposite Panama.


IV.  ACAPULCO, MEXICO

*The Acapulco panorama was probably taken from a hill located behind the city. The view would have incorporated a great portion of the old colonial part of town, including the fortress (presumably the Fortress of San Diego) and port facilities generally. It is possible that Vance was traveling on either the* Panama *or the* Sea Bird *during his trip northward.*

103  Panoramic View of Acapulco, from a hill back of the city, showing the City, Fort, Harbor, with the Steamers, Panama and Sea Bird, and others, lying at anchor.

104  Acapulco, from the Bay, showing a front view of the city and mountains in the back ground.


V.  STOCKTON AND STANISLAUS RIVER MINING REGION

*Stockton was at the head of navigation and a major access route to the southern mines via Knight's Ferry, a primary crossing point over the Stanislaus River (see pls. 113 and 114).*

11  Panoramic View of Stockton, from the top of Stockton House; showing the whole surrounding country.

12  View of Stockton House. *This was Stockton's first hotel, located on Weber Point as early as 1850.*

57   View of Indians on the Stanislaus River dressed for a war Dance.

58   Valley of Stanislaus River at Knight's Ferry.

59   View of Malones, on Carson's Creek, foot of Gold Mountain, in which is the richest
quartz vein in the world, one company alone taking out $25,000 per week! *Presumably
"Melones," Calaveras County, on the Stanislaus River about two miles south of the town of Carson
Hill. The* San Francisco Alta California, *June 16, 1851, makes reference to Meloney's Diggings.
There are a number of "Gold Hill" and "Gold Mountain" sites in the California goldfields.*[58]

60   Evening View at Knight's Ferry on the Stanislaus River.

61   Residence of Capt. Webber [Weber], at Stockton. *Captain Charles M. Weber started his first
store in Stockton in 1847. By 1850 he had built an elaborate home on land between McLeod's Lake
and the Stockton Channel. This became known as Weber Point.*

62   View of Indian Commissioners, Dr. Wozencraft, Col. Johnson [Johnston], Indian Agent,
and Clerks, in treaty with the Indians. *O. M. Wozencraft was appointed Indian Commissioner
in October 1850. Adam Johnston was the Indian sub-agent for the San Joaquin Valley. The treaty
negotiations mentioned were most likely those that occurred in mid-March 1851.*[59]

69   Indian Village on the Stanislaus River.

70   Indians, cooking.

71   View of Indians dressed for a Dance.

72   Indian, dancing.

118  Knight's Ferry (Stanislaus River).

VI.   SONORA AND MOKELUMNE MINING REGION

*Sonora, Tuolumne County, was settled in 1848 by Mexicans from the state of Sonora. The* San Francisco
Alta California, *March 1, 1852, recorded that in one week local banks received 3,412 ounces of gold.
Mokelumne Hill (Diggings, Gulch, etc.), Calaveras County, was one of the most important gold camps in
the Southern Mines (see pl. 49).*

51   Panoramic View of Sonora.

52   Holden's Garden at Sonora, from which the largest lump of Gold ever found, was taken,
weighing twenty-eight pounds. *Holden's Garden, Tuolumne County, is now a part of the Sonora
High School campus. According to one source, gold was originally found in Holden's vegetable garden
attached to the roots of a cabbage plant. In April 1851, the Holden's garden chispa was discovered:
a lump weighing more than twenty-eight pounds, twenty of which were estimated to be gold.*[60]

54   View of Main Street, Makelame [Mokelumne].

55   Panoramic View of Makelame [*sic*], with Ball Mountain in the back ground.

88   Mining Scene at Sonora.

VII.   VIEWS OF BENICIA

*Benicia, Solano County, was founded on December 26, 1846, as a logical place for "a metropolis of the
West." This was a major stopping point for eastbound vessels along the route to the goldfields. It was also
the site of a U.S. Army garrison and arsenal (see pls. 27 and 116).*[61]

93    Panoramic View of Benicia, showing the Straits of Carquines [Carquinez], on the opposite coast, Martinez Village, with the surrounding country, also the U. S. Barracks, Pacific Steam Navigation Company's works, etc.; this place is a port of entry, and destined to be a place of first importance as a commercial city.

94    View of Steamer Senator at the Wharf.

95    View of Steamer Confidence.

VIII.    SACRAMENTO AND ENVIRONS

*Sacramento (sometimes called the City of the Plain) was the most significant California settlement east of San Francisco (see pl. 112). Because Sacramento could be reached directly by maritime means, it was frequently the first supply point for miners bound for the diggings. The devastating floods of January 1850 led to the development of extensive levees along the riverfront. When Vance photographed these levees they were apparently already well established, thus suggesting a date following the winter rains of 1850–51 when the raw scars of levee building would have lessened. The town of Washington was located on the opposite bank of the Sacramento River, west of Sacramento.*

96    Jay Street, Sacramento City, from the levee.

120    Washington, from the levee, at Sacramento.

121    View of the Levee at Sacramento, taken from the South end.

122    Levee and River, from Washington, opposite.

123    Jay Street, Sacramento, from the top of the Hotel in 2d [Second] Street.

124    Panoramic View of Sacramento, with the surrounding country, giving a view of Washington, opposite separated by the Sacramento River.

125    Hotel, cor. of Second [and] Jay Street[s], from which the view of Sacramento was taken.

126    East and South View of Sutter's Fort. *Sutter's Fort was the early terminus of the emigrant trail from Missouri. In August 1839, pioneer John A. Sutter settled at the site that is now Sacramento. He began construction of his famous fort in 1841 (see pl. 55).*

127    North and East View of Sutter's Fort.

128    Part of First Street and Levee.

129    Portrait of Capt. Sutter. *It is not known whether Sutter's likeness was taken in Sacramento, or at Hock Farm, perhaps at the same time as view number 100.*

IX.    PLACERVILLE AND COLOMA MINING REGION

*Placerville, El Dorado County, ranks as the third most important mining location in California (after Sutter's Mill). Coloma, El Dorado County, was the site of Sutter's Mill on the south fork of the American River. It was here that James Marshall discovered gold on January 24, 1848, inaugurating the great California gold rush.*

42    Mining scene in a Street of Placerville.

43    Panoramic View of Placerville, from a Hill East of City; this being the first place of arrival for those crossing the Plains.

44    View of Coloma, from a Hill north of the place on the West side of the River.

45   Coloma; showing River and surrounding Country.

46   View of Capt. Sutter's Saw-Mill and Dam across the American River. *Site where Marshall found gold in the millrace of Sutter's Mill.*[62]

47   Rear View of the Saw-Mill Race, where the Gold was first discovered.

48   View of Main Street, Coloma, from the Court House.

49   Panoramic View of Coloma, from the East side of the River.

50   View of Coloma, from the West side of the River.

63   View of Hangtown [Placerville]. *Hangtown is considered an early name for Placerville.*

83   Mining Scene, at Placerville.

102  View of Hangtown.

X.    NEVADA CITY AND ENVIRONS

*Nevada City, Nevada County, grew at the site of a gold discovery in the fall of 1849. A network of water ditches was begun in 1850, and hydraulic mining ensued. The* San Francisco Evening Picayune, *September 16, 1850, reported the finding of a gold lump weighing upwards of 400 pounds, for which the finders refused an offer of $25,000.*

73   Miners at Work on Little Deer Creek, at Nevada [City].

74   View of Gold Run. *Gold Run, Nevada County, was a stream mentioned as early as August 26, 1849: "on the banks of Deer Creek and Gold Run." This site contained some of the richest and most famous diggings ever known in California.*[63]

80   View of Miners at Work near Nevada; showing the manner of washing gold with the Long Tom.

81   Miners at Work on Deer Creek; showing the manner of sluice washing.

82   View of Gold Run, a mining district near Nevada.

84 & 85   Views — Front and Back of a Saw-Mill, near Nevada, worked by mule power.

86   Panoramic View of Gold Run, so called from the rich gold diggings, it being one of the first places where gold was discovered, the gold lying at a depth of thirty feet from the surface.

87   Miners at Work at Gold Run. *Presumably not the Gold Run near Dutch Flat, later on the route of the Central Pacific Railroad.*

89   View of Central Street, from a height south of the city.

90   Main Street, Nevada.

91   View of Central Street, Nevada.

92   Panoramic View of Nevada City, with the surrounding forest; giving the enormous size to which the trees attain in this region, some of them three hundred feet in height, and twenty-seven feet in circumference.

XI.   YUBA CITY/MARYSVILLE AND ENVIRONS

*Yuba City was settled near the confluence of the Yuba and Feather Rivers. The town was laid out and named after the Yuba River in August 1849. Early settlement of Marysville, Yuba County, began in the fall of 1842, on land leased from John Sutter. The town was laid out in the winter of 1849–50 by Auguste Le Plongeon, a French-born surveyor. (Le Plongeon later practiced daguerreotypy in San Francisco and is the same man noted for his archaeological efforts in the Yucatán, Mexico.) Marysville was the important metropolis and supply center for the Feather and Yuba River mines (see pl. 25).*[64]

53   View of Yuba City, on the Feather River, mouth of the Yuba River.

56   Indian Hut near Yuba City.

64   Scenery of Yuba River near Marysville.

65   View of Indian Village on Capt. Sutter's Plantation. *Indian villages were frequent along the banks of the Sacramento and Feather Rivers. A major Indian village was situated at Hock Farm, John Sutter's farmstead and residence. Several sketches of these Indians survive from John Wesley Jones's Pantoscope of 1851; especially the illustration titled "Indian Rancheria — Hock Farm."*[65]

66   Indian Village near Yuba City.

67   View of four Indian Chiefs, and Wife and Sister of the celebrated chief Kasuse.

68   A group of Indian Chiefs on the Feather River.

97   View of Hock Farm, the residence of Capt. Sutter, on the Feather River. *Jones's Pantoscope includes a view of Hock Farm, titled "Hock Farm, Home of Captain John A. Sutter."*[66]

98   Hock Farm, from the East side of the River.

99   View of Hock Farm, from the top of the house and [showing] the celebrated Bute [Butte] Mountains, sixteen miles distant.

100  Residence of Capt. Sutter; Group in front, of the Captain, his Daughter and Son-in-law. *Although Captain Sutter's daughter, Eliza, did not marry until March 1852, she was engaged to a portrait painter named William Shaw shortly after March 1851 (she did not marry Shaw because of his ill concealed ambition to marry for wealth). Presumably the "Son-in-law" mentioned in Vance's caption is Shaw.*[67]

101  View of Levee at Marysville, and Steamers. *Marysville, like Sacramento, was easily reached by inland steamers (see pl. 25).*

110  Panoramic View of Marysville, California, from the top of the United States Hotel, giving a beautiful view of the surrounding country, with its forests of Oak.

111  Ferry at Marysville, on the Yuba River.

112  View of Main-st. [Marysville].

113  A California Theatre, at Marysville.

114  U. S. Hotel. *The U.S. Hotel underwent extensive remodeling in December 1850 before reopening as the largest hotel in Marysville. The Marysville Herald, February 28, 1851, advertised a daguerreian artist occupying rooms at this hotel until approximately April 1851. It is possible that Vance also occupied this room, either before or following the unnamed daguerreian's departure.*

115  View of West Side of the Square [Marysville].

116  [View] of South Side of the Square.

117  [View] of North Side of the Square.

XII.  SAN FRANCISCO PRIOR TO THE MAY 4, 1851, FIRE

*The pre–May 1851 views of San Francisco may have been taken at any point after Vance's arrival in California. During the actual exhibition, however, many of these pre-fire views were paired with images from the same vantage points but taken after the fires of May and June. Where the views have the same catalog number (and composite caption) they have been subdivided into "before" and "after" sequences for the purposes of this listing.*

1  Panoramic View of San Francisco, from the top of Union Hotel in Portsmouth Square. Showing the whole surrounding country, bay, and islands. *The* San Francisco Pacific Daily News, *November 5, 1850, advertised that the Union Hotel "will be opened for the reception of guests on Thursday, the 7th of November," also that the building had been "erected within the last three months" (see pl. 128).*

2  Views of San Francisco . . . [before] the May Fire, taken from the top of Russia [Russian] Hill, North of the City. *Russian Hill would have provided a sweeping view of San Francisco from the West.*

3  View[s] of Clay Street . . . [before] the Fire; taken from Dupont Street.

4  Views of Central Street . . . [before] the Fire; taken from Kearney Street.

5  View of California Street, between Montgomery and Sanson [Sansome] Streets.

6  Panoramic View of San Francisco, from the corner of Montgomery and Broadway Streets, before the May Fire, showing the bay and shipping, and Mission lands in the distance. *Presumably this panorama covered an east-south sweep, including Mission Dolores, which was almost due south.*

9  View of the West side of Montgomery Street, from Clay Street, before the May Fire.

13  Panoramic View of San Francisco, from Powell Street.

16  View of Telegraph Hill, from Union Hotel. *Telegraph (or Signal) Hill was another prominent lookout point, lying almost due north of Portsmouth Square.*

17  Views of Jackson Street . . . [before] the May Fire.

18  Views of Sacramento Street . . . [before] the Fire.

19  East Side of Portsmouth Square . . . [before] the Fire. *Portsmouth Square (or the plaza) was an important social and commercial center for San Francisco. The* San Francisco Alta California *newspaper office was situated here, as well as the Bella Union (a music hall) and various gambling halls (see pl. 35). During the 1850s many of the city's early photographers operated studio locations on the streets bordering the plaza.*

20  End of Central Wharf, and Shipping.

21  Bella Union — Sociedad and Louisiana Gambling Houses, on the North Side of Portsmouth Square.

22  View of Dupont Street, from Clay Street.

23  Merchants Street, and East side of Portsmouth Square; before the Fire.

[25] Views of Sanson [sic] Street . . . [before] the Fire. *This title apparently numbered "24" in error.*

26   Views of California Street . . . [before] the Fire.

27   Montgomery Street . . . [before] the Fire.

28   View of the End of Pacific Wharf.

29   View of Oriental Hotel. *The Oriental Hotel was built shortly after the Union Hotel, mentioned earlier.*

30   Part of Central Wharf, from Whitehall Hotel — East View.

31   West view of Central Wharf, from the same place [as no. 30].

32   West side of Portsmouth Square; before Fire. *Paired with another view "after the Fire," also numbered no. 3.*

33   South side of Portsmouth Square.

34   Cunningham's Wharf and Yerba Buena Island, in the Bay.

35   Stockton Street, from Clay Street.

36   Broadway, from Powell Street.

37   Washington Street, from Dupont Street.

38   Kearney Street, from Broadway; on Election day. *Presumably the first election of municipal officers, which occurred on April 28, 1851.*[68]

39   Panoramic View of San Francisco, from the top of Telegraph Hill; showing the entrance to the Bay, from the Ocean, the opposite coast of Sancelita [Sausalito], Angel Island, and the entrance to San Pablo Bay. *Telegraph Hill provided a perfect vantage point for points north of the city, including the "Golden Gate," the Marin County headlands and north shore of San Francisco Bay. Sausalito was a convenient place for maritime shipping because it was handy to fresh water and abundant lumber products.*

40   View of Telegraph Hill, from Clay Street.

41   View of Pacific Street.

75   View of Mission Church, three miles from San Francisco. This Mission, Delores [Dolores], now time-worn and crumbling to ruins, was a proud and influential religious establishment, of the days of the Jesuits, founded more than a century ago, and even up to the time of the deposition of the late government, was considered one of the most interesting Spanish Missions in the whole of California. *Construction of a "plank roadway" was begun in November 1850 to link the mission with Portsmouth Plaza, some two and a half miles away. Regular omnibus service commenced at this time (see also nos. 76 and 77).*[69]

76   Part of the Mission Church turned to a Hotel, with Green and Bowen's Omnibuses in front.

77   Spanish House near the Mission, with Omnibus in front.

78   Panoramic View of the Mission and surrounding country.

79   View of the Mission, taken from the hill south of the Church, showing the country between it and San Francisco. *This overview would be a remarkable document today. As far as I am aware, there are no distant photographs of San Francisco dating from the 1850s. For instance, nothing taken from the Marin Headlands, the Berkeley/Oakland hills, and so on.*

XIII.  SAN FRANCISCO AFTER THE MAY 4, 1851, FIRE

*The May 4, 1851, fire is called the* fifth *great fire to ravish San Francisco. By all accounts this fire was more invasive than all previous fires combined.*[70] *This series of "after" images is in the best tradition of a modern "rephotographic" project. Presumably Vance lost his gallery facilities in the fire, yet in no less than four days (or earlier), he was busy photographing the fire damage from many of his previous standpoints.*

2   Views of San Francisco . . . [after] the May Fire, taken from the top of Russia [*sic*] Hill, north of the City.

3   View of Clay Street . . . [after] the Fire, taken from Dupont Street.

4   Views of Central Street . . . [after] the Fire; taken from Kearney Street.

7   View of the Burnt District, from the corner of Montgomery and Broadway Streets; four days after the May Fire.

10  View of the same after the Fire. *Matches number 9 — View of the West side of Montgomery Street, from Clay Street, before the May Fire.*

14  Ruins of the City next day after the May fire, from the head of California Street.

17  Views of Jackson Street . . . [after] the May Fire.

18  Views of Sacramento Street . . . [after] the Fire.

19  East Side of Portsmouth Square . . . [after] the Fire.

24  Merchants Street; after the Fire.

25  Views of Sanson [*sic*] Street . . . [after] the Fire.

26  Views of California Street . . . [after] the Fire.

27  Montgomery Street . . . [after] the Fire.

32  West side of Portsmouth Square; after the Fire. *Matches a similar view also numbered "32" but taken before the fire.*

XIV.  SAN FRANCISCO AFTER THE JUNE 22, 1851, FIRE

*The June 22, 1851, fire was known as the* sixth *great fire. The six fires successively destroyed nearly all the old buildings and landmarks dating from the "Yerba Buena" period of San Francisco's physical history.*[71]

8   View of the Burnt District, from the corner of Montgomery and Broadway; after the June Fire. *Apparently taken from the same sites as number 6 (before May fire) and number 7 (after May fire).*

15  Ruins of the Burnt District, from Powell Street; after the June Fire.

## NOTES

1   Overview writings on the life and times of Robert H. Vance include: R. Bruce Duncan, "Gold Rush Photographer," *Graphic Antiquarian* 2 (October 1971): 14–19; Peter E. Palmquist, "Robert Vance: Pioneer in Western Landscape Photography," *American West* 18 (September/October 1981): 22–27; Peter E. Palmquist, "Silver Plates on a Golden Shore: 'The Real Thing Itself,'" in John Wood, ed., *America and the Daguerreotype* (Iowa City: University of Iowa Press, 1991), 134–58. For a discus-

sion on Vance's origins, see Peter E. Palmquist, "Robert H. Vance: The Maine and Boston Years (1825–c. 1850), *The Daguerreian Annual* (1991): 198–216.

2  Abel Alexander, "Robert H. Vance: Pioneer of the Daguerreotype in Chile," *The Daguerreian Annual* (1993): 11–30.

3  Vance's gallery sites included San Francisco, Marysville, and Sacramento, California; Virginia City and Carson City, Nevada; and Hong Kong.

4  Vance's death occurred in New York City at age fifty-one, and was "sudden." He was interred at Forest Grove Cemetery in Augusta, Maine.

5  For a fine overview of painted panoramas, see Robert Wernick, "Getting a Glimpse of History from a Grandstand Seat," *Smithsonian Magazine* 16, no. 5 (August 1985): 68–84. See also John Francis McDermott, "Gold Rush Movies," *California Historical Society Quarterly* 33 (March 1954): 29–38; likewise, Bertha L. Heilbron, "Making a Motion Picture in 1848," *Minnesota History* 17 (June 1936): 131–49.

6  Alexander, "Robert H. Vance," 20–23.

7  *Kennebec Journal*, March 24, 1848, 3.

8  Ibid., October 5, 1848, 3.

9  The pattern of Vance's *Views in California* is remarkably similar to Emmert's panorama, parts 3 and 4: The picture began with the crossing of Panama: "a bold view of the Castle of San Lorenzo—Chagres, with its harbor dotted with canoes. A full length view of the Chagres River . . . and a grand view of Panama." The second reel took the audience as far as Acapulco. On the way, one might see "a view of the suburbs of Panama from the French Hotel; Panama as seen from the bay [etc.]." Part 3 was devoted to San Francisco and the route to the goldfields; here was to be seen the "Entrance to the Bay of San Francisco (called the Golden Gate); City of San Francisco, with its beautiful harbor and shipping, — Happy Valley; City of Benecia; Sacramento River; Sacramento City." The final section pictured "Sutter's Fort; Mormon Island; Mississippi City; Hangtown; Culloma [*sic*] or Sutter's Mill; Spanish Bar; Big Bar, Volcanic Bar; Rector's Bar, Etc." McDermott, "Gold Rush Movies," 30.

10  Ibid., 29.

11  R[obert] H. Vance, *Catalogue of Daguerreotype Panoramic Views in California* (New York: Baker, Godwin, 1851), preface.

12  Ibid.

13  Cliff Krainik, "Cincinnati Panorama," *Graphic Antiquarian* 3 (April 1974): 7–12; see also R. Bruce Duncan, "Silver Plates on a Swampy Shore," *Graphic Antiquarian* 2 (July 1972): 10–17. The Cincinnati Panorama was first publicly shown in 1849 at the Franklin Institute in Philadelphia and received the highest award for a photographic image. It was also displayed at the Maryland Institute in Baltimore. In 1851 it was exhibited at the Crystal Palace, London. The work then disappeared until 1887, when it was briefly shown at Landy's Gallery. Once again it dropped out of sight. On January 11, 1911, the Chamber of Commerce Building of Cincinnati burned down, and among the smoldering ruins was found the panorama. Miraculously, the framed daguerreotypes had survived a plummet of three stories and the "destructive appetite of the flames."

14  McDermott, "Gold Rush Movies," 30.

15  Catherine Hoover, "Pantoscope of California," *California Historical Courier* ( July 1978): 3 ff. See also "Jones' Pantoscope of California," *California Historical Society Quarterly* 6 (1927): 109–238. Associated with Jones were California daguerreians William and Jacob Shew and Seth Louis Shaw.

16  Alexander, "Robert H. Vance," 26–28.

17  *San Francisco Daily Pacific News*, January 21, 1851.

18  Vance's large camera made whole plate daguerreotypes measuring 6½ by 8½ inches. While there may have been other photographers with cameras of this size, few San Francisco whole plate daguerreotypes survive today. It is likely that he used a smaller-format camera for his studio portraiture at this time.

19  Charles P. Kimball, comp., *The San Francisco City Directory* (San Francisco: Journal of Commerce Press, 1850).

20  *San Francisco Alta California*, January 1, 1853.

21  Ibid., March 15, 1851.

22  On March 9 an "indignation" meeting of several thousand persons gathered to consider the conduct of a local judge toward William Walker, one of the editors of the *San Francisco Daily Herald*. Reported in Frank Soule, John H. Gihon, and James Nesbit, *The Annals of San Francisco* (New York: Appleton, 1855), 322–24.

23  See John Walton Caughey, ed., "Life in California in 1849: As Described in the 'Journal' of George F. Kent," *California Historical Society Quarterly* 20 (March 1941): 30. "The [Steamer] Senator makes the passage up to Sacramento (a distance of about 150 miles) in 10 hours. the cabin fare is $25 (since raised to $30). The ordinary deck fare in schooners and boats is $12 or $14, cabin fare $20."

24  Vance is known to have inherited money from his father, and he probably accumulated additional wealth while in South America. Presumably, therefore, he could have afforded to hire help and may have done so, although no evidence survives to support this idea. Perhaps more to the point, none of the known daguerreians of the era has ever mentioned participating in Vance's panorama. It is reasonable to expect, however, that he had the assistance of a packer while transporting his cumbersome camera and supplies in the field.

25  McIntyre was a Florida dentist who took daguerreotypes in Tallahassee as early as November 1844. He had plans to duplicate his panorama and sell them to the public for $100. He apparently suffered heavy loss in the May 4, 1851, fire. In July 1851, the editors of *Humphrey's Journal* in New York received "a fine panoramic view of San Francisco" by McIntyre, which consisted of five half plate daguerreotypes in a side-by-side presentation, showing the span of the city and bay "from beyond Rincon Point to the hill surmounting the North Beach." In addition, the editors reviewed a collection of McIntyre's half plate views of the California goldfields. The matched set, housed in a single frame, included six studies of "all sorts" of miners at work: "men, with spade and tin pan in hand, eagerly looking after the *dust*; some examining a lump just found, others up to their knees in Water, and among the rest is, in a bent position, a man, pan in hand, looking up with a grin, exhibiting 'somcthing' in his pan which he no doubt would try to make us believe was the metal" ("Panorama of San Francisco and the Gold Diggins," *Daguerreian Journal* 2 [July 1, 1851]: 115–16).

26 *Alta California*, January 19, 1851.

27 *San Joaquin Republican*, June 18, 1851.

28 *Alta California*, April 19, 1851. None of Jones's daguerreotypes have been authenticated to exist today.

29 *The Annals of San Francisco*, 305.

30 Ibid., 605–6.

31 *San Francisco Daily Pacific News*, May 9, 1851.

32 Ibid., May 18, 1851.

33 The *Photographic Art-Journal* 2 (September 1851): 189, noted: "We have had among us, during the last month, quite a number of western and southern daguerreians, who have come eastward for the purchase of their winter's supply of materials [among them] . . . Mr. Vance of San Francisco." Details of the rosewood framing are found in the February 1853 issue of this same journal, p. 126.

34 *Humphrey's Journal* 2 (October 15, 1851): 340–41.

35 *Photographic Art-Journal* 2 (October 1851): 253.

36 *Humphrey's Journal* 1 (January 15, 1851): 148.

37 Vance, *Catalogue*, preface.

38 *Photographic Art-Journal* 2 (October 1851): 252–53.

39 *Daguerreian Journal* (November 1, 1851): 371.

40 Ibid. (October 1851): 253.

41 Ibid.

42 *New York Weekly Tribune*, June 21, 1851, devoted six columns to an account of the May 4 fire; a substantial coverage of the June 22 fire was published on August 6.

43 *Humphrey's Journal* 1 (1850): 49.

44 *Photographic Art-Journal* 5 (February 1853): 126.

45 Ibid. (March 1852): 195. Vance apparently retained ownership of his collection during the period while it appeared at Gurney's gallery. See the Fitzgibbon advertisement in Beaumont Newhall, *An Historical and Descriptive Account of the Various Processes of the Daguerreotype and the Diorama by Daguerre* (New York: Winter House, 1971), between figs. 14 and 15.

46 Beaumont Newhall, *The Daguerreotype in America* (New York: Duell, Sloan, and Pearce, 1961), 61.

47 *Photographic Art-Journal* 5 (February 1853): 126.

48 Ibid., 129.

49 Ibid. (July 1853): 53.

50 Ibid. (August 1853): 129.

51 *Missouri Republican*, May 1, 1854.

52 Ibid., April 8, 1854.

53 *Photographic and Fine Art Journal* 9 (April 1856): 128.

54 Dolores Kilgo, "Vance's Views in St. Louis: An Update," *The Daguerreian Annual* (1994): 211–12.

55 *American Journal of Photography* 6 (September 15, 1863): 143. This editorial comments on Fitzgibbon's difficulties during the Civil War, his lack of supplies causing him to flee St. Louis, etc., and quoting a Charleston newspaper's plea for silver in any form: "Silver Plate Wanted — To be con-

verted into caustic [silver nitrate] for the use of the sick of the army, $8 per ounce will be paid for all prime plate."

56 Millie Robbins, "Those Vanished Vances," *San Francisco Chronicle*, February 25, 1970. This article speculates that a recently (at that time) discovered Vance view of the "Excelsior Building," San Francisco, might have been part of the "Lost 300."

57 *Photographic Art-Journal* 5 (February 1853), 129, lists no. 119 as "A view." This article listed all of Vance's images for sale and is generally the same as his catalog titles.

58 Data from Erwin G. Gudde, *California Gold Camps* (Berkeley: University of California Press, 1975), 134–35, 212.

59 Annie R. Mitchell, "Major James D. Savage and the Tularenos," *California Historical Society Quarterly* 28 (December 1949): 328–31. *Humphrey's Journal* 2 (November 1, 1851): 371, also commented on the Indian commissioners, "in treaty with the Indians, presenting a fair likeness of the natives and the above named gentlemen as they are in a field." Also, "Landscape and view of Indians in and about the wigwams."

60 Gudde, *California Gold Camps*, 158.

61 Erwin G. Gudde, *California Place Names: The Origin and Etymology of Current Geographical Names* (Berkeley: University of California Press, 1969), 26.

62 For an extensive survey of Sutter's Sawmill, see *California Historical Society Quarterly* 26 (June 1947): 107–62.

63 Gudde, *California Gold Camps*, 136.

64 Gudde, *California Place Names*, 194, 371–72; also, *California Gold Camps*, 209.

65 "Jones' Pantoscope of California," *California Historical Society Quarterly* 6 (June 1927): 109–253.

66 Ibid.

67 James Peter Zollinger, *Sutter: The Man and His Empire* (New York: Oxford University Press, 1939), 306–7.

68 Soule, Gihon, and Nesbit, *The Annals of San Francisco*, 325–26.

69 Ibid., 296–98.

70 Ibid., 329–33.

71 Ibid., 344–47.

# The Plates

1
Unknown maker
**Nisenan Indian Man with Arrows**
Sixth plate daguerreotype
Courtesy of the Southwest Museum, Los Angeles

2

Robert H. Vance (1825–1876)

**Captain William H. Richardson, Builder
of the First House in San Francisco**

Half plate daguerreotype
Collection of the California State Library

3
Unknown maker
**George Baumford in Buckskins
and Suspenders**
Quarter plate daguerreotype
Collection of Matthew R. Isenburg

4
Frederick Coombs (1803–1874)
**Ferry *Erastus Corning*, San Francisco Bay**
Quarter plate daguerreotype
Courtesy San Francisco Maritime National Historical Park

5
William Shew (1803–1874)
**Chilean Sailor, Jumped Ship in San Francisco Bay**
Ninth plate daguerreotype
Collection of Stanley B. Burns, M.D.

6
Unknown maker
**Panorama of San Francisco, 1851** (detail)
Whole plate daguerreotype from six-plate
panorama
Collection of the California Historical Society

7
Unknown maker
**Thomas Drew, Forty-Niner**
Two sixth plate daguerreotypes
Collection of the Society of California Pioneers

8
Unknown maker
**Miners with Rocker and Blue Shirts**
Half plate daguerreotype
Collection of W. Bruce Lundberg

9
Unknown maker
**Mining Claim on Mathenas Creek, 1850**
Half plate daguerreotype
Collection of Leonard A. Walle

10
Unknown maker
**Young Forty-Niner with Shovel and Pan**
Quarter plate daguerreotype
Collection of Leonard A. Walle

11
Unknown maker
**An Evening Scene, Boston Flat, Calaveras County**
(**Miner Playing the Flute by His Cabin**)
Half plate daguerreotype
Collection of the Society of California Pioneers

12
Unknown maker
**Two Miners with Gold Nugget Stick-Pins**
Quarter plate daguerreotype
Collection of the Oakland Museum of California,
Prints and Photographs Fund

13
Unknown maker
**Miners in Rocky Stream Bed**
Half plate ambrotype
Collection of Stephen Anaya

14
Unknown maker
**Young Gent** (**Miner with Plaid Pants**)
Quarter plate daguerreotype
Collection of Carl Mautz

15
Unknown maker
**Mining Scene at Grizzly Flat, Placer County**
Half plate daguerreotype
Collection of the Bancroft Library

16
Unknown maker
**James Warner Woolsey, Nevada City, with
Nugget Weighing over Eight Pounds**
Sixth plate daguerreotype
Collection of Mrs. Vivienne Bekeart

17
Unknown maker
**Four Miners and the Town of Volcano,
Amador County**
Quarter plate daguerreotype
Collection of the Bancroft Library

18
Unknown maker
**Street Scene in Eureka or Trinidad, Humboldt County**
Quarter plate ambrotype
Collection of Peter E. Palmquist

94

19
Unknown maker
**Men Moving a Steam Boiler**
Half plate daguerreotype
Collection of the Society of California Pioneers

20
Unknown maker
**R. Lowe's Miners' Tent Store**
Quarter plate daguerreotype
Collection of Stephen Anaya

21
Unknown maker
**Armstead Calvin Brown, Assemblyman and Judge,
in His Office, Jackson, Amador County**
Whole plate ambrotype
Collection of Charles Schwartz

22
Unknown maker
**Wells Fargo Office, Iowa Hill, Placer County**
Half plate daguerreotype
Collection of the California Historical Society

23
Unknown maker
**F. A. Hornblower's Miners' Store, Unidentified Town**
Quarter plate daguerreotype
Collection of Matthew R. Isenburg

24
Unknown maker
**Morgan & Brother's Store and Wells Fargo Office,**
**Unidentified Town**
Quarter plate daguerreotype
Collection of Leonard A. Walle

100

25
Unknown maker
**The Levee at Marysville, Yuba County**
Half plate daguerreotype
Collection of the Oakland Museum of California,
Museum Income Purchase Fund

26
Unknown maker
**Smith's Exchange, Natoma Valley, Sacramento County**
Half plate daguerreotype
Collection of the Bancroft Library

27
Unknown maker
(possibly George Howard Johnson)
**The Wharf at Benecia, with Sunken Ship**
Half plate daguerreotype
Collection of Stephen Anaya

28
Unknown maker
**Miners Working under Sluice Network**
Half plate daguerreotype
Collection of the Bancroft Library

29
Unknown maker
**Joseph Sharp, Miner**
Sixth plate ambrotype
Collection of the Bancroft Library

30
Unknown maker
**Elmer Bliss and Partners at Mining Claim**
Half plate daguerreotype
Collection of the Bancroft Library

31
Unknown maker
**William McKnight, Died in California**
**on August 12, 1852**
Sixth plate daguerreotype
Collection of Matthew R. Isenburg

32
Unknown maker
**Brothers Visiting California Grave of Solomon Hartshorn**
Half plate daguerreotype
Collection of Stanley B. Burns, M.D.

33
Unknown maker
**"My dear brother who sailed for California and
who has never returned"**
Ninth plate oval daguerreotype in locket
Collection of Graham Pilecki

34
Unknown maker
**View of San Francisco, 1853**
Six whole plate daguerreotypes in vintage frame
Collection of the Oakland Museum of California,
Museum Founders Fund

35
Unknown maker
**Portsmouth Square Before the Fire
of May 4, 1850**
Sixth plate daguerreotype (image laterally
reversed in original)
Private collection

36
Frederick Coombs (1803–1874)
**Charles Minturn, Steamboat Entrepreneur**
Half plate daguerreotype
Courtesy San Francisco Maritime National Historical Park

37
Seth Louis Shaw (1816–1872) and George
Howard Johnson (c. 1823–?)
**Smith & Porter's Coffee House, San Francisco**
Whole plate daguerreotype
Collection of the Bancroft Library

38
Unknown maker
**Captain John Henderson and Friend**
Half plate daguerreotype
Collection of the California Historical Society

39
Isaac Wallace Baker (1810–c. 1862)
**Chinese Man**
Sixth plate daguerreotype
Collection of the Oakland Museum of California,
gift of anonymous donor

40
Unknown maker
**San Francisco and the Bay**
Half plate daguerreotype
Collection of Greg French

41
William Shew (1820–1903)
**Offices of the *San Francisco Evening Picayune* and
the *San Francisco Herald***
Half plate daguerreotype
Collection of the Bancroft Library

42
Unknown maker
**Banking House of James King of William, San Francisco**
Whole plate daguerreotype
Collection of Wells Fargo Bank

43
Robert H. Vance (1825–1876)
**Sacramento Street, San Francisco, During the**
**Vigilante Uprising, 1856**
Whole plate daguerreotype
Collection of the Bancroft Library

44
Unknown maker
**San Francisco Fire Brigade #2 on Meiggs' Wharf**
Whole plate ambrotype
Collection of the Bancroft Library

45
Unknown maker
**Mary Elizabeth Beatty Walker**
Sixth plate daguerreotype
Collection of the Oakland Museum of California,
gift of Mrs. Reginald Walker

46
Jacob Shew (1826–1879)
**Boy and Girl in Costume Dress**
Quarter plate daguerreotype
Collection of Robert Harshorn Shimshak

47
Robert H. Vance (1825–1876)
**Rix Family House, Market Street, San Francisco,**
**August 20, 1855**
Whole plate daguerreotype
Collection of the Oakland Museum of California,
Museum Program Fund #757

48
Isaac Wallace Baker (1810–c. 1862)
**Baker in Front of Batchelder's Daguerreian Saloon**
Quarter plate daguerreotype
Collection of the Oakland Museum of California,
gift of anonymous donor

49
Unknown maker
**Daguerreotype Studio, Mokelumne Hill, Calaveras County**
Half plate daguerreotype
Collection of W. Bruce Lundberg

50
Attributed to William Herman Rulofson
(1826–1878)
**William Herman Rulofson Displaying
a Paper Photograph**
Half plate ambrotype
Collection of the California State Library

126

# Pre-Discovery

*For a few brief years, in far off California, the bottom fell out of the nineteenth century.*
— *Kevin Starr*

51
Isaac Wallace Baker (1810–c. 1862)
**Native Californian**
Sixth plate daguerreotype
Collection of the Oakland Museum of California,
gift of anonymous donor

52
Unknown maker
**Hispanic-American Plaza, Probably Near Alviso,
Santa Clara County**
Whole plate daguerreotype
Collection of the Oakland Museum of California,
the David M. Faraday Collection,
gift of Kathleen C. Faraday and
Jeffrey Michael Faraday

*In the hands of an enterprising people, what a country this might be!
Yet, how long would a people remain so in such a country? If the
"California fever," laziness, spares the first generation, it is likely to
attack the second. — Richard Henry Dana*

53
Unknown maker
**Andreas Pico, Commander of the Californio Forces Against**
**the Americans at the Battle of San Pasqual**
Quarter plate daguerreotype
Collection of the Seaver Center for Western History Research,
Natural History Museum of Los Angeles County

54
Unknown maker
**María Rosalia Vallejo Leese, Sister of Mariano**
**Vallejo and Wife of Jacob Leese**
Quarter plate daguerreotype
Collection of the California Historical Society

55
Unknown maker
**Captain Sutter (John Augustus Sutter, on Whose
Land Gold Was First Discovered)**
Quarter plate daguerreotype
Collection of the California State Library

56
Attributed to Mathew Brady Studio
**John C. Fremont, "Pathfinder of the West"**
Whole plate daguerreotype (possibly copy plate)
Collection of the Oakland Museum of California,
Museum Founders Fund

# Gold!

57
Gabriel Harrison, New York (1818–1902)
**"California News"**
Half plate daguerreotype
Collection of Gilman Paper Company

*The fact is, this last gold news has unsettled the minds
of even the most cautious and careful among us.*
— New York Express, *January 1849*

58
Unknown maker
**George W. Northrup, Minnesota**
Quarter plate daguerreotype
Collection of the Minnesota Historical Society

*A frenzy seized my soul; piles of gold rose up before me at every step; thousands of slaves bowed to my beck and call; myriads of fair virgins contended for my love. In short I had a violent attack of gold fever.*
— *Anonymous soldier*

59
Henry E. Insley, New York (c. 1811–1894)
**Charles B. Curtiss Before Leaving for California, 1849**
Sixth plate daguerreotype
Collection of Carl Mautz

60
Unknown maker
**Charles B. Curtiss in Mining Clothes**
Sixth plate daguerreotype
Collection of Carl Mautz

*Poets, philosophers, lawyers, brokers, bankers, merchants, farmers, clergymen — all are feeling the impulse and are preparing to go and dig for gold and swell the number of adventurers to the new El Dorado.*
— New York Herald, *January 11, 1849*

# Leaving Home

*I have got to leave here, and perhaps shall do better [in California] than elsewhere.*

— *Daguerreotypist Richard Carr*

61
Unknown maker
**Young Forty-Niner with Rifle and Shovel**
Quarter plate daguerreotype
Collection of Stephen Anaya

62
Unknown maker
**"Going West"** (**Charles W. Cox and Walter Brewster with Their Wagon, Battle Creek, Michigan**)
Quarter plate daguerreotype
Collection of Matthew R. Isenburg

*Ho for California! — Common slogan*

63
Unknown maker
**E. Deane About to Leave for California**
Sixth plate daguerreotype
Collection of John McWilliams

*I have bought a trunk for $3 with two straps on it. I have priced all the rifles in town and find that I can get one that will answer for about $15 and good revolvers at the same price. I have had my likeness taken and cased for $2 and shall send it to Sabrina . . . with a token of fond remembrance.*
— *William Swain, forty-niner*

# By Sea

*Descriptions of a "life on the ocean wave" read very prettily on shore, but the reality of a sea voyage speedily dispels the romance.*
— *Samuel C. Upham, brig* Osceola

64
Albert Sands Southworth (1811–1894) and
Josiah Johnson Hawes (1808–1901)
**Ship in Dry Dock, Boston Navy Yard**
Whole plate daguerreotype
Collection of the George Eastman House

65
Unknown maker
**Members of a Mining Company, Sailed for California on the Ship *Roe***
Whole plate daguerreotype
Collection of the Society of California Pioneers

*Our voyage is becoming prolonged to an excessively wearisome duration. . . . We suffer much from weariness, lassitude, and drowsiness, consequent on our long voyage and almost total inactivity.*
— *J. Lamson, passenger on the* James W. Paige, *August 1849*

66
Unknown maker
**Valparaiso, Chile**
Whole plate daguerreotype in vintage frame
Collection of Matthew R. Isenburg

*I fear the morals of Valparaiso are not of the highest order. Yet a more social,
hospitable, and polite people I have never met.*
— *L. M. Schaeffer, passenger on the* Flavius, *bound for California*

# Overland

*Any man who makes a trip by land to California deserves to find a fortune.*

— *Alonzo Delano, forty-niner*

67
Unknown maker
**Dr. MacBeth in the costume in which he
crossed the plains, fleeing from the cholera, of
which he died**
Half plate daguerreotype
Collection of the George Eastman House

68
Unknown maker
**The Garvas Tharrow House with Covered Wagon,**
**Eagleswood, New Jersey**
Quarter plate daguerreotype
Collection of Matthew R. Isenburg

69

Alexander Hesler (1823–1895)

**U.S. Mail Packet** *New St. Paul* **and Steamboat**
*Nominee* **at Galena, Illinois**

Half plate daguerreotype

Collection of the Chicago Historical Society

70
William C. Mayhew
**The Sitgreaves Expedition,** *1850*
Half plate daguerreotype
Collection of R. Bruce Duncan

*Expect to find the* worst desert *you ever saw & then find it worse than you* *expected. Take water,* be sure to take enough.
— *Note left on the trail*

71
Thomas M. Easterly (1809–1882)
**Nacheninga or No-Heart of Fear, 1849**
Quarter plate daguerreotype
Edward E. Ayer Collection, Newberry Library

72
Unknown maker
**Indian Village, Minneapolis**
Half plate daguerreotype
Collection of the Minnesota Historical Society

# Arriving

*SAN FRANCISCO: "A beautiful country, romantic scenery, excellent harbor, a fine climate and plenty of game — this is the place for me," thinks I, upon sighting land. "It is the most degraded, immoral, uncivilized and dirty place that can be imagined, and the sooner we are away from here the better for us," thinks I, five minutes after being landed on shore. — Daguerreotypist Isaac Wallace Baker*

73
Unknown maker
**Warehouse on Wharf, San Francisco**
Whole plate daguerreotype
Collection of W. Bruce Lundberg

74
Unknown maker
**Panorama of San Francisco, 1851** (detail)
Whole plate daguerreotype from a six-plate panorama
Collection of the California Historical Society

*I emerged into a bed of* mud, *anywhere from ankle deep to "off soundings."*
*I looked, found 'twas no use, put my trousers inside my boots and started.*
*— Daguerreotypist Isaac Wallace Baker*

75
Unknown maker
**"Sarah Anne MacDougal with Elizabeth,
January 1850, Upon Arrival in California"**
Quarter plate daguerreotype
Collection of Joan Murray

*You may rest assured that I have an older head on my
shoulders by about 1,000 years than when I left the states.
— William Wells, forty-niner, October 21, 1850*

# In the Diggings

*Looking upon these pictures, one can almost imagine himself among the hills and mines of California.*

— Photographic Art-Journal, *1851*

76
Attributed to Joseph Blaney Starkweather
(c. 1822–?)
**Miners at Spanish Flat, El Dorado County**
Quarter plate daguerreotype
Collection of the California State Library

77
Unknown maker
**Henry Barnhisel of Amador County**
Half plate ambrotype
Collection of John McWilliams

78
Unknown maker
**Gold Miners at Dig**
Half plate daguerreotype
Collection of the George Eastman House

*Panning is exceedingly laborious and taxes the entire muscles of the frame. . . . The abundance of gold in California has not been as much overrated as the labor of procuring it has been underrated.*
*— William McCollum, Jacksonville*

79
Unknown maker
**Group of Miners in a Ditch**
Quarter plate daguerreotype
Collection of Matthew R. Isenburg

80
Unknown maker
**Miner with Pick and Suspenders**
Half plate daguerreotype
Collection of W. Bruce Lundberg

81
Unknown maker
**George Ellis and His Ore Cart**
Sixth plate daguerreotype
Collection of the Oakland Museum of California,
gift of Stanley B. Burns, M.D.

82
Unknown maker
**Anable Placer Mine, Auburn, Placer County**
Quarter plate daguerreotype
Collection of the Bancroft Library

83
Unknown maker
**Mary A. McCloskey**
Sixth plate daguerreotype
Collection of the Huntington Library

84
Unknown maker
**Six Miners in Rocky Terrain**
Quarter plate daguerreotype
Photographic History Collection, National
Museum of American History, Smithsonian
Institution

# Life in the Mines

85
Unknown maker
**"Our California Home," Vallecito, Calaveras County**
Half plate daguerreotype
Collection of California Department of Parks and
Recreation, Sutter's Fort State Historic Park

86
Unknown maker
**French Miners at Lunch**
Quarter plate daguerreotype
Collection of Matthew R. Isenburg

87
Unknown maker
**Six Miners in Front of Their Log Cabin**
Half plate ambrotype
Collection of W. Bruce Lundberg

*A mixed and motley crowd — a restless, roving, rummaging, ragged*
*multitude never before reared in the rookeries of man.*
*—Anonymous*

88
Unknown maker
**"Gold Dust Wanted"** (**Miners with Cabin**)
Half plate daguerreotype
Collection of Marc and Mona Klarman

*In no country of the world have I found so much selfishness
and such immense love of money as in this El Dorado.*
— *Heinrich Schliemann*

89
Unknown maker
**Woman with Bonnet**
Sixth plate daguerreotype
Collection of Peter E. Palmquist

*Got nearer to a female this evening than I have been
for six months. Came near fainting.*
— *Young miner, Nevada City*

90
Unknown maker
**Group of Miners in Front of a Barracks**
Half plate daguerreotype
Collection of W. Bruce Lundberg

91

Isaac Wallace Baker (1810–c. 1862)
**Isaac Wallace Baker (left) and a Friend
Playing Poker**
Quarter plate ambrotype
Collection of the Oakland Museum of California,
gift of anonymous donor

*Gambling, drinking and* houses of ill fame *are the chief amusements of this country. Therefore you see that we have nothing but work, reading and writing to amuse us, as we are all nice young men and do not frequent such places. — Lucius Fairchild, miner, 1850*

92
Unknown maker
**Pair of Fiddlers**
Quarter plate tintype
Collection of the Bancroft Library

*I have seen purer liquors, better segars, finer tobacco, truer guns and pistols, larger dirks and bowie knives and prettier courtesans than in any other place I have ever visited. California can and does furnish the best bad things that are available in America.*
— Hinton Rowan Helper

93
Unknown maker
**F. M. Failing and C. D. Brown,**
**Sacramento Masons**
Sixth plate ambrotype
Collection of Peter E. Palmquist

# Boom Towns

94
Unknown maker
**Street in Tent City, with Miner and His Family**
Half plate daguerreotype
Collection of the Amon Carter Museum
P1988.1

95
Isaac Wallace Baker (1810–c. 1862)
**Murphy's Camp, Calaveras County, July 1853**
Quarter plate daguerreotype
Collection of the Oakland Museum of California,
gift of anonymous donor

96
Unknown maker
**Orlando Ballou with Mule**
Half plate ambrotype
Collection of Gary W. Ewer

97
Unknown maker
**Miner Street, Yreka, Siskiyou County**
Quarter plate daguerreotype
Collection of the Siskiyou County Museum

98
Unknown maker
**Mining Town (Possibly Rough and Ready,**
**Nevada County)**
Half plate daguerreotype
Collection of W. Bruce Lundberg

99
Unknown maker
**Michigan Bar, El Dorado County**
Half plate daguerreotype
Collection of the Society of California Pioneers

*The perfumes of pork and slapjacks arising from a hundred frying pans could only be compared with all the soap factories in Ohio frying out at full blast. — William Downie, Bullards Bar*

100
Unknown maker
**Unidentified Town with Miners Digging in Street**
Half plate daguerreotype
Collection of the Henry Ford Museum and
Greenfield Village, B51784

176

101
Robert H. Vance (1825–1876)
**James D. Parker, Miner, 1853**
Quarter plate daguerreotype
Collection of the Oakland Museum of California,
Museum Income Purchase Fund

102
Unknown maker
**James F. Freeman Standing in His Wagon,**
**Marysville, March 1855**
Half plate ambrotype
Collection of the Bancroft Library

103
Unknown maker
**The National Hotel, Forbestown, Butte County**
Half plate ambrotype
Collection of the Bancroft Library

104
Unknown maker
**Unidentified Mining Town**
Half plate daguerreotype
Collection of the University of New Mexico Art Museum,
purchase through the University of New Mexico
Foundation, Inc.

105
Unknown maker
**Overview of Mining Town, with Cloudy Sky**
Half plate daguerreotype
Collection of the Bancroft Library

# Loneliness and Separation

*I received your daguerreian. . . . I think I never saw anything but life look more natural. I showed it to Little Cub, and to my astonishment and pleasure she appeared to recognize it. She put her finger on it, looked up at me and laughed, put her face down to yours, and kissed it several times in succession. Every time it comes in her sight she will cry after it.*

*— Sabrina Swain to her husband in California*

106
Unknown maker
**"The Family Daguerreotype"**
(**Woman Holding a Whole Plate Daguerreotype**)
Sixth plate daguerreotype
Collection of the George Eastman House

107
Unknown maker
**Four Miners Reading a Letter**
Quarter plate daguerreotype
Collection of Matthew R. Isenburg

*If you could have seen us when we received our letters, you would have laughed and perhaps called us fools —such hoorahing, jumping, yelling and screaming. . . . You will take good care and write often when I tell you that I live upon your letters, with a small sprinkling of pork and bread.*
*— Miner from Wisconsin*

108
William Shew (1820–1903)
**Young Man Writing a Letter**
Sixth plate daguerreotype
Collection of the Bancroft Library

*This long anxious waiting for news is one of the most corroding cares that trouble me.*
*— Miner from Illinois to his wife*

# Business and Commerce

109
Unknown maker
**Miners' Tent Store**
Half plate daguerreotype
Collection of Matthew R. Isenburg

*Money is our only stimulus and the getting of it our only pleasure. Never was any country so well calculated to cultivate the spirit of avarice.*
*— Miner from Missouri*

110
Unknown maker
**Diamond Spring, El Dorado County, 1854**
Half plate daguerreotype
Collection of the California Historical Society

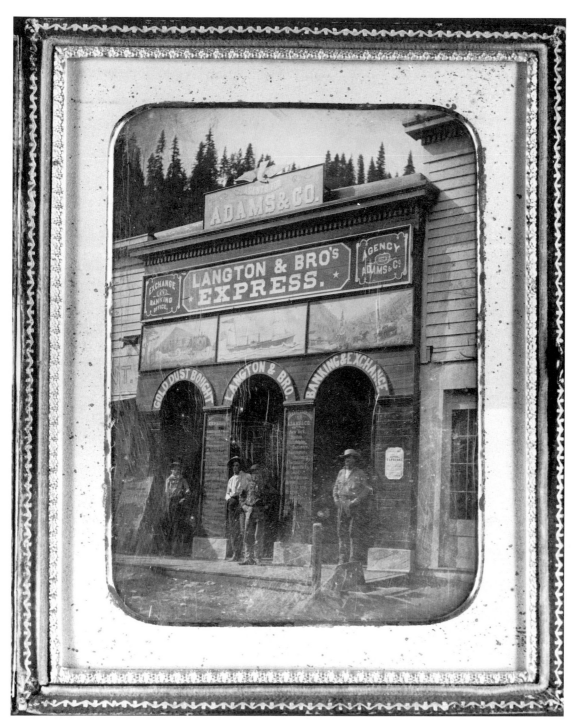

111
Unknown maker
**Express Company Offices, Downieville, Sierra County**
Half plate daguerreotype
Collection of the Society of California Pioneers

# Supply Centers

112
George Howard Johnson (c. 1823–?)
**Fourth and J Streets, Sacramento**
Whole plate daguerreotype
Collection of the Bancroft Library

113
Attributed to William Herman Rulofson
(1826–1878)
**Stockton Channel and the Steamboat *Sagamore*, Stockton**
Half plate daguerreotype
Collection of the Family of Helen Weber Kennedy

114
Attributed to William Herman Rulofson
(1826–1878)
**The Corinthian Building and Stockton Channel, Stockton**
Half plate daguerreotype
Collection of the Family of Helen Weber Kennedy

115
Robert H. Vance (1825–1876)
**Stage Stop and Freeman Crossing**
Half plate daguerreotype
Collection of the J. Paul Getty Museum

116
Unknown maker
**Street in Benicia, Solano County**
Half plate daguerreotype
Collection of Stanley B. Burns, M.D.

# Industrialized Mining

*Views of Mining Claims, Flumes, Etc., taken at short Notice and on favorable terms.*
*— Daguerreotypist Oliver H. P. Norcross*

117
Isaac Wallace Baker (1810–c. 1862)
**Miners and Sluice Boxes**
Quarter plate daguerreotype
Collection of the Oakland Museum of California,
gift of anonymous donor

118
Attributed to Joseph Blaney Starkweather
(c. 1822–?)
**Coyote and Dear Creek Water Company**
Quarter plate daguerreotype
Collection of the California State Library

119
Unknown maker
**Hydraulic Mining, Placerville,**
**El Dorado County**
Half plate daguerreotype
Collection of the Oakland Museum of California,
the S. H. Cowell Foundation

120
Attributed to William Shew (1820–1903)
**Miners in Rocky Diggings**
Half plate daguerreotype
Collection of the Bancroft Library

*All the varieties of mining life pass before us, and all the processes of mining. Nay, we see the very identical miners who were at work when the views were taken, in the very attitudes of real work; for they kept their positions for a time, by request, that the daguerreotypes might fix them for ever. — Eastern writer*

# Illness and Mortality

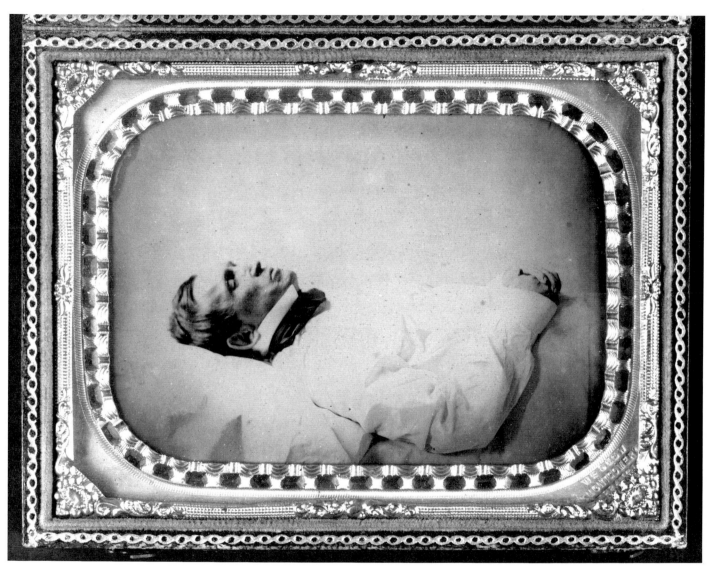

121
William Shew (1820–1903)
**Postmortem Portrait of Middle-Aged Man**
Quarter plate ambrotype
Collection of Peter E. Palmquist

*Secure the shadow ere the substance fade.*
*— Daguerreian advertising slogan*

122
James May Ford (1827–c. 1877)
**Grave of Robert Barnard, Died 1856**
Half plate daguerreotype
Collection of the New-York Historical Society

123
Unknown maker
**Young Widow, Clutching a Daguerreotype**
Ninth plate ambrotype
Collection of the Bancroft Library

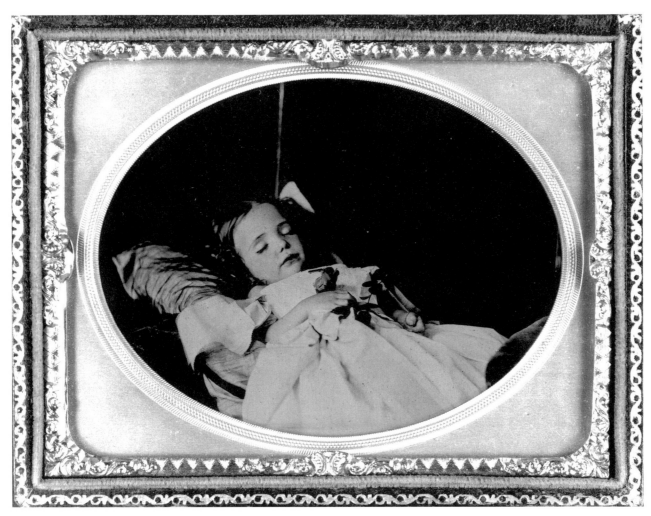

124
Charles F. Hamilton (c. 1823–?)
**Postmortem Portrait of Eloise Channing**
Quarter plate ambrotype
Collection of the Bancroft Library

125
Unknown maker
**California Mining Cemetery**
Half plate daguerreotype
Collection of W. Bruce Lundberg

126
Robert H. Vance (1825–1876)
**Mother and Child in Mourning**
Quarter plate daguerreotype
Hallmark Photographic Collection,
Hallmark Cards, Inc., Kansas City, Missouri

127
Unknown maker
**California Grave of Phillip A. Potter**
Whole plate daguerreotype
Collection of Matthew R. Isenburg

*Suicides caused by disappointment are as numerous as the deaths resulting from natural causes. — Forty-niner*

# Instant Metropolis

*One of the best collections of curiosities with which returning Californians could supply themselves, would be the different engravings and daguerreotypes of San Francisco, taken at various stages of her progress.* — San Francisco Herald, *1851*

128
Unknown maker
**The Union Hotel under Construction, San Francisco**
Half plate daguerreotype
Collection of the Metropolitan Museum of Art, David Hunter McAlpin Fund, 1949 (49.111)

129
Unknown maker
**Four Northern California Carpenters**
Sixth plate daguerreotype
Collection of Robert Harshorn Shimshak

130
Frederick Coombs (1803–1874)
**Montgomery and Clay Streets, San Francisco**
Half plate daguerreotype
Collection of the George Eastman House

131
Unknown maker
**Eleven Men with Beards, Top Hats, and Vests**
Half plate daguerreotype
Collection of the Oakland Museum of California,
gift of Concours d'Antiques

*You cannot know the perfect freedom and independence
that characterizes all our relationships. . . . Society if it
exists at all is freed from the multitude of prejudices and
embarrassments and exactions that control the Eastern
cities. — Lawyer John McKrackan*

132
Silas Selleck
**Hulett's Tailor Shop, San Francisco**
Quarter plate daguerreotype
Collection of Matthew R. Isenburg

133
Frederick Coombs (1803–1874)
**John B. Newton in Overcoat and Hat**
Quarter plate daguerreotype
Hallmark Photographic Collection,
Hallmark Cards, Inc., Kansas City, Missouri

*I am in an odd humor but in San Francisco one has an*
*undoubted right to be . . . it is an odd place.*
— *San Francisco resident*

# California Culture

134
Unknown maker
**The First Baptist Church Built in San Francisco,
Washington Street**
Whole plate daguerreotype
Collection of the Huntington Library

135
Unknown maker
**Fulton, the Actor**
Sixth plate daguerreotype
Collection of the Bancroft Library

136
Unknown maker
**Lola Montez (?), Actress, Dancer, and Courtesan**
Sixth plate ambrotype
Collection of the Bancroft Library

137
Attributed to James May Ford (1827–c. 1877)
**Matilda Heron, Actress**
Quarter plate daguerreotype
Collection of Peter E. Palmquist

138
Unknown maker
**South Park, San Francisco**
Whole plate daguerreotype in vintage frame
Collection of the Oakland Museum of California,
Museum Founders Fund

# Women and Family

*The arrival of every steamer brings the wives and families of our most respected citizens.*

*Such a thing as* HOME *is becoming known in San Francisco!*

— San Francisco Picayune

139
Robert H. Vance (1825–1876)
**Young Woman in Off-the-Shoulder Gown**
Sixth plate daguerreotype
Collection of Carl Mautz

140
Unknown maker
**Fred Stocking, His Bride, Lucinda Stocking,**
**and His Partners, Big Oak Flat, Tuolumne County, 1856**
Half plate daguerreotype
Collection of the Oakland Museum of California,
gift of Concours d'Antiques

141
James May Ford (1827–c. 1877)
**Young Woman in Bonnet**
Sixth plate daguerreotype
Collection of Peter E. Palmquist

142
Robert H. Vance (1825–1876)
**Wedding Portrait**
Half plate ambrotype
Collection of Peter E. Palmquist

143
Jacob Shew (1826–1879)
**Daughter of Serranus Clinton Hastings**
**of Hastings Law School**
Half plate daguerreotype
Collection of the Bancroft Library

144
William Shew (1820–1903)
**Governess and Child**
Quarter plate ambrotype
Collection of the Society of California Pioneers

# Vigilantes!

*How many murders have been committed in this city within a year?*

*And who has been hung or punished for the crime? Nobody!*

— *Editorial,* San Francisco Alta California, *1851*

145
Robert H. Vance (1825–1876)
**James King of William, Editor and Banker,**
**Whose Murder Roused the Vigilance Committee**
Quarter plate daguerreotype
Collection of the Oakland Museum of California,
Prints and Photographs Fund

146
Unknown maker
**Sharpshooters of the 1856 Committee
of Vigilance**
Whole plate ambrotype
Collection of the Oakland Museum of California,
gift of the S. H. Cowell Foundation

147
Unknown maker
**Parade of the Second Committee
of Vigilance, San Francisco, 1856**
Whole plate daguerreotype
Collection of the New-York Historical Society

148
Robert H. Vance (1825–1876)
**"The Great Man Has Fallen"** (**Funeral Procession**
**of James King of William**), **San Francisco, 1856**
Whole plate daguerreotype
Collection of Gilman Paper Company

# Photography in California

149

Attributed to William Shew (1820–1903)

**Shew's Daguerreian Saloon and the *Alta California* Newspaper Office, San Francisco, 1851**

Half plate daguerreotype

Collection of the Oakland Museum of California, gift of Mr. and Mrs. Willard M. Nott and Dr. Paul S. Taylor by exchange

*A good deal of curiosity has been expressed in regard to the object and intention of the big wagon which fills up a large portion of the Plaza. . . . Some suppose that "the elephant" which so many people come here to see was to be caged up in it and exhibited to greenhorns at a quarter a sight — others that it was to be a travelling rum mill, and a variety of other things. It seems, however, that it is to be a travelling daguerreotype establishment, with which the proprietor intends to travel around the city and country, taking views and portraits.* — San Francisco Alta California, *1851*

150
Unknown maker
**Daguerrean Studio Above Store, Unidentified Mining Town**
Half plate daguerreotype
Collection of Greg French

*Those wishing to have a good likeness are informed that they can have them taken in a very superior manner, and by a real live lady too, in Clay St. opposite the St. Francis Hotel. . . . Give her a call gents.*
*— Daguerreotypist Julia Shannon*